Writing *Short Stories*

Writing

Short Stories

The Most Practical Guide

William H. Phillips

 Syracuse University Press

First Edition 2002
02   03   04   05   06   07   6   5   4   3   2   1

The paper used in this publication meets the minimum requirements of
American National Standard for Information Sciences—Permanence of
Paper for Printed Library Materials, ANSI Z39.48–1984.∞™

Library of Congress Cataloging-in-Publication Data
Phillips, William H., 1940-
    Writing short stories : the most practical guide / William H. Phillips.—1st ed.
        p. cm.
    Includes bibliographical references and index.
    ISBN 0-8156-2919-2 (alk. paper)-ISBN 0-8156-2944-3 (pbk. : alk. paper)
        1. Short story—Authorship. I. Title.
    PN3373.P432001
    808.3'1—dc21   2001034194

Manufactured in the United States of America

para mi amiga,
amor,
y esposa—
para solamente una persona—
Eva

When writers make us shake our heads with the exactness
of their prose and their truths, and even make us laugh
about ourselves or life, our buoyancy is restored. We are
given a shot at dancing with, or at least clapping along
with, the absurdity of life, instead of being squashed by it
over and over again. It's like singing on a boat during a
terrible storm at sea. You can't stop the raging storm, but
singing can change the hearts and spirits of the people
who are together on that ship.

—Anne Lamott

*Bird by Bird: Some Instructions
on Writing and Life*

William H. Phillips is a continuing visiting professor of English at the University of Wisconsin-Eau Claire. His publications include *St. John Hankin: Edwardian Mephistopheles* (1979), *Analyzing Films* (1985), *Writing Short Scripts,* 2d ed., (Syracuse University Press, 1999), and *Film: An Introduction* (2d ed., 2002).

Contents

Figures

Preface

This book was written for four types of readers: individuals who want to begin writing short stories on their own, people who already write stories on their own, writers who meet with other writers to read and critique each other's work, and students in introductory or intermediate creative writing courses. No matter which type of reader you are, if you follow the specific and practical guidance in this book and work at your writing, you can write effective stories. If you absorb the information and apply the suggestions, and work really hard, you can likely write excellent ones. Many earlier drafts of this book were used in creative writing courses and by writers groups, then revised in response to reader reactions and requests. The book's examples and stories originated from individual students and their writing groups and were then group-tested and rewritten for later use.

During my twenty-two years of teaching university-level creative writing courses, I have seen that effective short stories are based on events that the writers know well and can re-create vividly: for beginners, largely their own experiences; for more experienced writers, experiences they know well, though not necessarily only their own. To help you capture some of those experiences in writing, this book shows you how to do writing exercises and write journal entries as you study a variety of short stories. Next, the book describes the fiction writer's major goals and the main components of short stories, using examples from the three stories included earlier in the book. Finally, the book illustrates how you might plan, write, and rewrite (and rewrite) your stories, then seek readers and publishers.

Thanks to Mike Henderson, Trita Stotts, and Jessica Barksdale Inclán—former students of mine who write short fiction and now teach—for their feedback on earlier drafts of the manuscript. I am also indebted to all my past creative writing graduate assistants whom I taught and who, in turn, taught me. Most of all, I want to thank Professor Eva L. Santos Phillips, who encouraged me to start this book and finish it. She has been my muse, mate, and gracious, supportive taskmaster.

Part One

Exploring Sources

Telling a story to convey feeling and experience is . . . as natural to man and as vital to man, and as intuitive and ageless . . . as to embrace when in love and to flee when in fear.

—Robert Crichton,
in *Creativity and the Writing Process*

1. General Sources

Good story ideas can come from anywhere . . . but the best
can be plucked from the family tree. More than fodder for
amusement, these stories bring relatives and friends closer
together and are a bridge between generations. "When an
old person dies," Alex Haley once told the national
storytelling league, "it's like a library has burned down."

—Dirk Johnson, "A Storytelling Renaissance"

Experience

Although professional writers often write effective stories that are based
heavily on in-depth research into a subject, you should base your first short
stories largely on either your own experiences or experiences you know
about in detail.

Often you know more about your own experience than you think you
do. All you need to do is write truthfully about what happened. As you
write and rewrite, forgotten memories often come pouring forth. David
Huddle writes,

when you sit down to write, you discover that *one thing leads to another,* and that in the act of writing, you can recover many fragments
of your life that have been lost to you; you can begin to recover
whole chunks of your history. "It's all back there somewhere," one of
my informed friends told me, tapping the back of his head. If you
think about that bedroom curtain, you remember, of course, that it
was green, that it had a musty smell, . . . that your mother made it,

that she made matching bedspreads for you and your brother, and that you would stand beside the sewing machine and talk with her sometimes while she worked . . . and, and, and" (Huddle 1982, 106–7; final ellipses are Huddle's).

I have seen countless students, and other writers, write effective stories based on experiences they know well. One beginner's story, for example, focused on the tensions among a lonely and protective mother, her daughter who lives at home yet goes to college and works part-time, and the daughter's boyfriend, who is eager for her to move in with him. The writer knew the material firsthand and presented it vividly and convincingly. In another example, a male author could give his story convincing details about the powerful, mostly sexual feelings a young man felt for an attractive young woman and about his insecurity, awkwardness, and possessiveness, which finally alienated her.

Use experiences and people that show something engaging about life. Begin with character and story, and let the meanings emerge from them. Do not begin with a message then look for the characters and story to illustrate it. Rarely does a writer begin with an idea—for example, that a person can be both good and evil simultaneously—then write a vivid and convincing story. Beginning with an idea usually results in a story that is too obviously written to make a point, rather than a story with the believable illusion of significant experiences from life.

Most of the stories based on people and events that have not been part of the beginning writer's life fail. Especially unlikely to have vivid and convincing details are stories based on people significantly older, of the opposite sex, or in an occupation or lifestyle unfamiliar to the writer.

A student once showed me an outline for a story about a business executive, an airplane pilot, and a flight attendant who survive a plane crash. In conference, I asked him what experience he had as a business executive, pilot, or flight attendant and when he had survived a plane crash. When he replied that he had no such experiences, I asked him where his story's words, ideas, and images would come from. I told the student that I suspected his language and images would come from television and movies, perhaps vaguely remembered.

What is wrong with using television and movie sources? The material is probably not true-to-life and, even if the material is effective, you will probably outfit it in the wrong clothing and spoil the effect. Without thorough knowledge of your subject—gained either by direct experience or through detailed knowledge of another's experiences—your story will quickly show only a passing acquaintance with its subject. You may not realize this until you've invested much time and effort and become increasingly unwilling to abandon a story doomed at conception.

Movies, television shows, and media stories are usually poor sources for your first short stories: they describe experiences that you do not know well and probably could not make your readers believe. For example, I once read a newspaper account of a man who killed a young man and woman, then was caught and convicted. The fathers of the murdered man and woman were witnesses at the execution. At the last moment, the murderer asked them for their forgiveness. One father nodded his head, indicating that he forgave. The other did not. This experience could be included in a larger, powerful story showing the consequences of both forgiveness and the inability to forgive. Few writers, however, even professional ones, could take this incident from the newspaper, incorporate it into a story, and make us entirely believe it. The story would lack convincing details. Using media accounts for story sources will likely not work because such accounts often deal with situations whose causes and consequences you may not understand. You might collect fascinating media accounts, and occasionally draw from this well for details in your stories, but beginning writers should generally avoid media stories as primary sources.

You should also avoid stories that have gratuitous violence or extraneous sexual situations. One day, I was walking in Central Park when I heard shouts and swearing, turned my head, and saw a heated argument. Even in New York, where loud confrontations are not unheard of, the argument stopped a few people and drew stares. Five minutes further into my walk in the park, I saw a couple lying on the grass, embracing and kissing. That, too, is a common sight, but it attracted attention. Violence, or the threat of violence, and sex both attract attention. You know that, and storytellers have long known it. The key is to use violence and sex only if they are consistent with your story's characters.

This caution also applies to profanity and obscenity. If they are appropriate to the characters and situation, use them. But remember that many readers believe that profanity and obscenity are verbal violence. In *Three Genres*, Stephen Minot compares sex and violence to electrical voltage: too much in a frail wire can burn it out. The shorter the story, the less tension it can carry without turning into melodrama, soap opera, or unintentional comedy.

One beginning writer's early draft described inner-city gang warfare.

The story focused on a gang of four young men. Two of the gang members kill two rival gang members in a shoot-out, then die in a head-on crash with a bus. Later, two of the rival gang members locate a member from the original gang of four and kill him. (The body count is now five.) With so many characters and so much violence in so short a piece (a mere $5^1/_2$ single-spaced pages), readers didn't get to know any of the characters well. The story also lacked vivid, believable details. Because of its excessive violence and lack of convincing details, the story failed to pull in readers and make them believe the story, let alone hold their attention. Choose the wrong source and you have a dead fish on your hands: you may be able to prettify it or briefly mask its hopeless condition, but you cannot bring it to life.

Avoid using recent experiences because you could lack a clear understanding of them. Ken Macrorie advises, "If you are under twenty, you need . . . to write of childhood. A writer requires some distance between him and the events he recalls—not always, but usually. Then he is unfamiliar enough with them to feel the need to relate them fully for his readers and for himself. If he writes of yesterday's or last year's events, he usually remembers them so well he leaves them shrouded in his nearby intimate memory, which the reader does not share" (Macrorie 1980, 116–17). The death of a loved one or a divorce or a separation, for example, can be excellent subjects *if* enough time has passed to allow you to understand the experience in its complexity and with some objectivity. If you write about a recent experience, you may not select the most significant events or omit insignificant details. You may also take it personally when readers give you their responses to the characters.

You should probably also avoid daring or dangerous experiences such as murders, attempted murders, suicides, car chases, explosions, pistol shots, acrobatics on moving trains, even fistfights. These actions are commonplace in action movies and commercial television, but they would be out of place in your first, more personal short stories, which should be based on experience and life as it is lived outside movie theaters and away from television screens.

Another type of experience that is an unsuitable subject for your story: unbelievable happenings. What if you read a short story about a woman who is shot during a holdup and, as the doctors prepare her for surgery, the bullet, which passed through a fur coat and three sweaters, falls out? Soon after, as the woman's mother rides a subway home, she overhears a fourteen-year-old boy boasting that he had recently shot a woman. The mother follows the youth from the train into a restaurant, where she calls the police.

Although the boy disappears after the police arrive, the mother later finds him while searching the streets, and the police arrest him. It turns out that one of the police officers arresting the youth lives next door to the family whose daughter has been shot! It's true ("Talk" 8).

Such events happen. We have all had incredible experiences, and we know of other unbelievable ones. And it's tempting to use those events in stories because they are fascinating. But if they are presented in a fictional story, they will be doubted. As the newspaper account above illustrates, truth is often stranger than fiction; truth is often harder to believe. You must tell a story that readers will believe, one that does not distract them with questions about its likelihood. It's futile to defend an improbable story you wrote by saying, "but it really happened." The fact that something happened doesn't matter. The fact that it will be believed as a story does matter.

Occasionally a story—or the beginning of one—falls right into your lap. Once, when my wife and I were out to dinner, a woman with a loud and distinct voice sat at the next table with her male companion. The woman's voice overwhelmed our own attempts at conversation. We could move, ask her to speak less loudly, or listen. She seemed like an articulate and intelligent person, so we listened. Soon this woman was engaged in an animated reunion with an old female friend who happened to have been seated at an adjacent table—her back to the first woman—with her own male companion.

The two women embraced warmly and talked fondly and enthusiastically. They had shared many experiences. At one point, the two men chatted for a while. Eventually, the second couple left. Before they were out of the room, the first woman announced, "That's her third husband." We then learned about all three husbands. We learned that the second woman always drank too much and got surly. She was, we heard, a demanding friend who asked too much of a friendship. "To tell you the truth," the first woman said, "I've been avoiding her." And on and on. During all this, my wife and I occasionally mouthed words at each other and tried to hide an occasional spasm of laughter, but mainly we listened with rapt attention. Later, I told my wife that the film we were on our way to see would likely be less entertaining than what we had just seen and heard.

A short story, or a major part of one, was there for the taking. It could be called "Reunion" and would have at least three scenes: (1) the first woman with her male companion, (2) the two women talking, then the second couple leaving, and (3) the first woman's reports to her male companion.

Perhaps the story should include some of the conversation that the two men had engaged in briefly while the two women talked warmly. Perhaps the story should include an eavesdropping couple and the effect that the overheard story had on them! Perhaps the first woman noticed the eavesdropping couple and spiced up her account a bit for their benefit. Probably, though, the focus should be kept on the first woman. When such good sources come our way, the first draft must be written at once—the next day may be too late—because the experience is not your own and you will soon forget the details needed to bring the story to life and keep it breathing.

When choosing sources, there are yet other pitfalls. For example, although dogs can seem human, avoid using a dog as a major player in a story (I've yet to see a beginner's story in which a dog is featured prominently that doesn't present a sentimental idealization or a preposterous humanization of the dog). You should guard against idealizing or glamorizing any subject. No one is perfect; no major character should be. If you base a major character on a person about whom you remember only positive traits, add at least one less-than-ideal fictional trait to the character.

Another form of idealization and simplification occurs if you base your story—knowingly or not—on commercial television shows or popular movies. In the following adaptation from a draft of a story, two high school students, Peters and George, have gotten into trouble and been summoned to the principal's office. There they quickly notice a new female student:

> "If you want, Mister Johnson, I'll show her around. Me and Peters have history this period."
> "Peters and I."
> "Yeah, all of us. My teacher's used to us roaming around . . ."
> "All right. Just stay out of trouble, and don't do anything stupid."
> "Of course," they replied.
> George and Peters left the office, leaving Mr. Johnson at his desk, wondering exactly when he lost control of his school.

The boys are so flippant and so in charge of the situation that the principal seems to forget why he summoned them in the first place. He even lets them continue to miss their history class to show the new student around. Then, too, the boys are incredibly familiar with the principal, and he seems unbelievably awkward and ineffective. Where would one find such a scene, except on a television sitcom or in a popular movie aimed at adolescent audiences? It's a scene that would be pleasurable for teenagers to fantasize about, but it is not of this life.

A final warning about sources. If you want to write fiction, don't present only anecdotes. An anecdote is a short entertaining story that lacks complexity. To see the difference between fiction and anecdote, read Allen Lujan's story in chapter 3, then contrast that version with the following version of an extract from it:

At the end of the alley, the man and I stopped in front of a back gate to a house. He opened the gate.

"This is home," he said. "Come on in." He pushed his bike into the backyard. I remained outside the gate, holding the bag of groceries.

"I need to go now," I said, as I bent over to set the groceries next to the gate.

"Nonsense," he said. "Bring that bag on in here. You're in no hurry. You said so yourself."

I stood up straight and remained outside the gate. "Honest, Mister. I got to go."

"My name's Pappy. You don't have to call me *mister*. What's your name?"

"Nick," I said.

"Well, come on in, Nick. I ain't going to bite you." He smiled.

"OK," I said. "But only for a minute."

I stepped past the gate and into the backyard. I held the bag and looked around the backyard while he parked his bike up against the side of the garage. I noticed a large garden, a dirt—and dust-covered boat, a clothesline stretched across a small patch of grass, a bird feeder, a bird bath, a large tree, a covered patio, and a few car parts scattered around. He walked around behind me and closed the gate.

"I don't want my boys to escape," he said, as he walked over to the door leading into the garage. The door was open. He stuck his head into the garage and hollered: "Charlie Brown! Feather! Come here, boys!" He turned and looked at me.

"Not too long ago, a young man jumped my fence and tried to steal the radio off my picnic table. You know what happened?" he asked. I shook my head. "My boys chewed him up a little bit and chased him right back over the fence. . ." As I was about to drop the groceries and make a run for the gate, out of the darkness of the garage emerged two old, scroungy dogs.

Both dogs squinted as they slowly, lazily crept into the backyard. One was a black-and-gray German shepherd, with patches of hair missing from his hind end. The other, a black mutt, about the same size as the German shepherd, walked with a limp. Its right front leg was almost useless. The dogs came over to me and began to sniff my shoes and pants legs.

I looked at Pappy. He was smiling. "Don't make a move," he said. "They're liable to attack." I looked at the dogs and shook my head. These were the two most helpless-looking dogs I had ever seen. The dogs continued to sniff my legs. I looked up at Pappy. He broke into loud laughter.

In this version, I have omitted the passage in which Pappy tells Nick that the dogs are adroit at sniffing out and attacking a thief. I have also omitted some of the details about Nick's nervousness as well as what comes before this point in the story and what comes later. This anecdote is too short, and too lacking in telling detail, to show much about Nick's and Pappy's personalities. Although the anecdote is concise and entertaining, it recounts only the major physical action and lacks the complexity and subtlety of effective fiction.

In summary, your short story should originate from a believable yet significant experience you have had that is not too recent. It should avoid unnecessary dangerous and violent actions, unmotivated and irrelevant sexual material, and excessive profanity and obscenity. It should also be more complex and subtle than an anecdote. Oh, and your story should be about something that you care about or are fascinated with. You'll probably end up spending more time on it than you ever imagined you would.

Imagination

Although your story should begin with an experience you know well, it should never end there. You must transform the experience into a fictional story. A story should be neither one hundred percent experience nor one hundred percent imagination. It should be a blend of the two (Figure 1). Until you are an accomplished writer, it's dangerous to write a story that is made up of less than fifty percent of your experience. You need to know

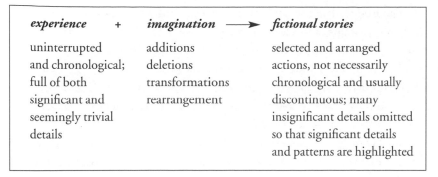

experience +	imagination	⟶	fictional stories
uninterrupted and chronological; full of both significant and seemingly trivial details	additions deletions transformations rearrangement		selected and arranged actions, not necessarily chronological and usually discontinuous; many insignificant details omitted so that significant details and patterns are highlighted

Figure 1. Making fictional stories

your main character and the situations thoroughly. If you don't, you are wasting everyone's time.

Often, during conferences, students show me a few scenes that are based on an experience, but the students don't know how to develop those scenes into a story. A student once showed me an episode based on material she knew well. A man who is separated from his wife leaves her and their children after a visit. Soon after, one of the young daughters accidentally sets fire to a curtain, then denies it. The mother questions each child separately. When the guilty girl's turn comes, she finally admits the deed. The writer presented the events vividly, but the story was only an anecdote, not effective fiction.

I suggested that the student change the names of the characters to fictional ones and that she consider the following possibilities: What if you show that the girl started the fire because she was distracted by thoughts of her father? What if she started the fire because she was angry about, and preoccupied with, her parents' breakup for which she feels partly to blame? What if the father returned after the girl's confession and treated the incident as unimportant because he believed it would ingratiate him with his daughter and annoy his wife? What if the daughter saw through the father's strategy and came to the defense of her mother? What if the other children were angry with the girl because her initial denial caused them to suffer an awkward cross-examination from their mother and they wanted to get even? What if the mother overreacted to the burned curtain because she was upset (the father's presence upset her, maybe being a single parent was getting her down, perhaps she still loved the man and wanted him back)? What if the mother said she forgave the daughter, but showed, by her actions, that she was either still angry or preoccupied with the father?

I suggested that the student add some of these possible actions to the original anecdote and show or suggest the causes and consequences of burning the curtain. Additional significant actions and dialogue from the family would show more about them and let us readers discover some of their complexities. The writer has only to ask "What if. . . ?" then consider what might be revealed about the characters. (For another example of playing "What if. . . ?" see chapter 7.)

To begin gaining perspective on an experience, it often helps to change the names of the people and to make other changes, such as omitting a person or adding an incident that didn't happen. The writer is then more likely to create fiction than to report life.

Fragments of autobiography rarely make satisfactory stories. Life is too unfocused; its significance often unclear; its minute-to-minute events too humdrum to keep readers involved. Alfred Hitchcock supposedly said that drama is life with the dull bits left out. Successful writers know to cut, transform, and rearrange events, and to change and invent characters and actions. No wonder fiction can be so special. It can reveal more to us, show it in sharper focus, and do so more quickly than can life itself.

Before you write anything, consider *when* you should write. You should write when you are rested. "Giving up as little as one night's sleep seriously undermines the mental skills of spontaneity, flexibility and originality that enable people to change perspective and break out of established thought patterns" (Stevens 1989, B7). Write when you are rested. Writing demands the best you have.

You should write during your productive time: in the morning if you are a morning person, or in the evening if you are a night person. If you are a morning person, try getting up every morning at least thirty minutes early and writing without talking to anyone, reading anything, listening to the radio, or watching television. If you are a night person, try to write for at least thirty minutes each night without interruption.

Writing after doing exercise can also be productive. For Joyce Carol Oates, running is integral to her writing: "Running! If there's any activity happier, more exhilarating, more nourishing to the imagination, I can't think what it might be. . . . The structural problems I set for myself in writing, in a long snarled, frustrating and sometimes despairing morning of work, for instance, I can usually unsnarl by running in the afternoon. On days when I can't run, I don't feel 'myself'; and whoever that 'self' is I feel, I don't like nearly so much as the other. And the writing remains snarled in endless revisions" (Oates, 1999). Because exercise can stimulate creativity, before your day exhausts you, run, jog, walk, swim, lift weights, or do some other exercise. Chuck Loch, a psychologist who has studied writers' creativity, says, "Anything physically repetitive, distracting or slightly boring will do" (Loch 1981, 21).

While you exercise, you may experience a surge of images, ideas, and energy; you may find memories and feelings you thought were lost. If ideas for writing come to you as you exercise, you can (1) try to remember what you want to write, (2) carry along a tape recorder or (3) stop exercising and write. It can be a hard choice, but that choice is much better than lacking something to write about.

2. Particular Sources

Belle McKensie, the creative-writing teacher, had fiery red hair and shapely legs the boys remarked on outside of class, and she had loud concepts of democracy and equality that she practiced when her temper didn't interfere. One student, named Hughes (I think), had moved to West Seattle from Oklahoma. . . . Hughes was shy, a stranger, just one of many of the 2,000 students passing through, unnoticed, lonely, and probably miserable.

One day he read aloud a theme he had written—we had to read our work aloud to get credit. It was a true story about an evening some older boys had taken him to a whorehouse. He had been fourteen at the time, and he was candid about his fears, his attempts to appear courageous and confident to the older boys, his eventual panic and running away. We were a bit apprehensive when he finished. That story could have gotten him thrown out of most classes in the school. McKensie broke the silence with applause. She raved approval, and we realized we had just heard a special moment in a person's life, offered in honesty and generosity, and we better damn well appreciate it. It may have been the most important lesson I ever learned, maybe the most important lesson one can teach. You are someone and you have a right to your life.

—Richard Hugo,
The Triggering Town: Lectures and Essays on Poetry and Writing

Writing Exercises

Performing writing exercises can sharpen your observing and writing skills as well as help you find material for stories.

Your responses to the ten writing exercises below should be kept in your journal or notebook and reread from time to time, but generally not immediately after you have written them.

1. Focused freewriting. Write quickly and spontaneously about an experience you have had or know well. As you write, record whatever comes to mind, without worrying about sentence structure, grammar, spelling, or capitalization. Don't worry about the possible usefulness of what you scribble. Above all, don't judge what you write or try to rewrite it as you write. Don't worry; simply write. When your attention begins to lag, rest only briefly, then write some more.

If you freewrite on a computer, try turning off the monitor or turning down the brightness so much that you cannot see what you are writing. That way, you are less likely to be distracted. You are also less likely to be drawn to negative thoughts and less likely to want to rewrite or correct as you write. Negative thoughts and rewriting while you write strangle creativity.

When you finish, put this exercise in your journal but do not look at it for a few days. When you read the exercise, you may find effective passages or you may not, or at least you don't think so now.

This exercise may help you tap into your unconscious, the well of most effective imaginary writing. You can never predict how productive focused freewriting will be. And you may do this exercise for a week or two and become convinced it is a waste of time. For most writers, though, the exercise eventually produces some effective writing. Some writers use it when they have trouble getting started—or restarted—writing.

2. Write everything you can remember about an experience that made you react with emotion: anger, jealousy, sadness, longing, pride, whatever. Describe the location, sounds, and events of the experience. What happened? Write the details without much planning. When you finish, put the passage aside for a day. The next day, reread it and add details that come to mind. Finally, rearrange the material into chronological order.

3. If you have a family photo album or set of slides, look at them. Choose photos that evoke strong feelings. Write about one of them: What was happening? What did it look like? What did it sound like?

As you look and look at a photograph and write, forgotten memories may flood your mind. Your past may live again. Write it all down without revising; later you can decide if any of it might be useful in a story. If it doesn't seem so now, put this exercise into your journal and look at it again another day.

4. One day when I was about twelve, I was riding my bicycle near the old drawbridge entry into the port of Corpus Christi, Texas. Near the water's edge and three feet below the edge of the sand sat two of my friends. I pedaled toward them at top speed, approached the edge above their heads, shouted to them, slammed on the bike's brakes—and flew right over their heads into the shallow water. The bike frame was bent; a watch my father had given me was torn from my wrist and lost; and I was soaked, confused, and trembling. From that experience I gained a sudden and deep-felt realization: I was subject to the laws of nature, jarring surprises, indignity, injury, even death—especially if I acted recklessly. After that, my life did not seem so charmed.

Choose an experience that taught you something, either about yourself or about another person you know well. Or choose a series of closely related events that changed you. Possible subjects: the time you learned you are more (or less) violent or impatient or poised or whatever than you had thought; or a time you became disillusioned with someone.

Do not describe and analyze the experience, as I did in my account about the bike, but re-create it in words. Be sure to give specifics. Where did it happen? How? With what consequences? Show, don't tell.

After you have written a first draft, read it aloud at least twice and revise it.

5. Choose an experience about which you have mixed feelings, such as love and hate, joy and sadness, fear and excitement, desire and disgust, exhilaration and depression, or anger and forgiveness. Change the names of the people involved and re-create the experience through one or more scenes of action and dialogue.

As you revise this exercise, remember that a scene is usually part of a larger action. For example, a scene showing a couple breaking up should not contain every word of their final conversation, only enough of it to show or hint at what is happening. After you have written the scene, you will probably discover that you need to do some pruning, especially from the beginning or ending, or both.

6. Imagine two tense characters having a dialogue. Show that tension through dialogue and action, not through physical attacks.

After the first draft, rewrite the dialogue: take out unnecessary words and sentences; reword phrases. Then, where needed, add descriptions of gestures and indications of tone of voice. Be sure that the indications of tone of voice are necessary: beginning writers often explain how characters say their lines when the dialogue itself already suggests how the lines are said. Your dialogue should seem natural yet be more compressed, engaging, and revealing than real conversation. Above all, it should show what the characters are like.

After you have done two or more drafts of the dialogue, consider having someone read one part aloud and someone else read the other. As you listen, take notes. Then revise.

7. Write a scene that shows three people you know well either in conflict or under pressure. Be sure to indicate what they do and what they say, but do not reveal what they are thinking or how you might feel about them.

Now change names, possibly change the order of events, omit unnecessary details, and add specifics. The result should be a scene with believable actions and dialogue.

Revise the scene, then file it in your journal or notebook.

8. Secure permission from two or three people to tape-record their conversation for half an hour. Next, transcribe five to ten consecutive minutes of the most revealing and engaging part of the conversation. From the transcription, choose a couple of pages that best convey their personalities. Lastly, rewrite, condense, and focus the conversation so that it conveys much in few words and yet still seems natural.

Some writers eavesdrop on people, then re-create those dialogues. Others consider that an invasion of privacy. You decide.

9. Write a scene without dialogue or the thoughts of the characters. Be sure to include only *concise* descriptions of locations, actions, and—perhaps—times.

10. Make lists of such items as, for example, your best friends, your worst enemies, places you have lived, things discarded or hidden in the attic or basement, attributes of your parents, and cars you have owned or driven. On different occasions, reread your lists and add details to some of the items. From Allen Lujan's "List of Every Car I Ever Owned": (1) '42 Plymouth (with suicide doors), (2) '69 Dodge Charger, (3) '76 Ford Courier ($3,600 new), (4) '62 Chevy pickup (step side), (5) Chevy station wagon, (6) Chevy Impala, (7) '62 Mustang (convertible), (8) Datsun pickup, (9) Chevy Luv pickup, (10) Datsun Roadster, (11) GMC pickup, (12) Kawasaki 450 (motorcycle), (13) Chevy Vega, (14) '85 Mercury, (15) '78 Toyota pickup, (16) '78 Cadillac.

Journals

One of the best ways to capture your experiences and imagination in words is to keep a journal or notebook and write in it nearly every day. If you use a loose-leaf binder, entries can easily be entered, taken out, rearranged. If you write with a computer, you can store your printouts in a loose-leaf binder. When composing either writing exercises or journal entries, which are described below, be sure to skip every other line so you'll have room to add and rewrite. Some writers crowd what they're saying onto the pages, leaving no room to rewrite, then *don't* rewrite. After all, there's no room! Don't allow yourself that excuse.

Below is a sample journal entry that was written by one of my former students:

Journal #10 Revised: "Stranded" by Karen Moody

I sensed trouble before I left San Carlos. The car had been heating up, so I stopped at a service station and had it looked at. It was about 10:30 p.m., and the kid who was pumping gas couldn't tell me much except that he thought it would be OK.

At the time, highway 238 was a bit isolated. I got about halfway to highway 17 when steam started pouring out from under the hood. I pulled over. It was dark, unfamiliar territory. I didn't often drive alone at night, especially not this far from home. I'd often wondered what I'd do if my car broke down while I was alone at night. It seemed that I was about to find out. I rolled up the windows and started to cry. The crying helped, but it didn't take long to realize that I still had a problem. I think that I had hoped that a highway patrol officer would hear my sobs and stop.

I looked around tentatively and noticed some old buildings across the road. Could there be a phone? I got out of my car and tried to get a better look, but from the distance it appeared dark and deserted. I got back in the car and locked the doors but not before I caught someone's eye.

The guy stopped, got out, and approached my window. He had a long scruffy beard, a biker's jacket and in general didn't resemble my vision of Prince Charming. At the moment he was one of the scariest people I'd ever seen.

I quickly thought of all the "to do" lists I'd ever read and found "What to do when you are stranded on a dark, lonely road, close to nowhere and all alone."

I rolled the window down a crack and mumbled, "If I give you a dime, will you call the Highway Patrol?"

"What'd ya say?"

My mind did a quick assessment of my situation. I could ask for the Highway Patrol again, but something told me he couldn't figure out why I would do that. I looked at him and the lack of traffic and knew that if he wanted to get me, he was capable of breaking a window.

I got out, mumbled something about vapor lock and opened the hood at his request. It was dark, and we couldn't see much.

"Do you have a flashlight?" he asked.

"In the trunk," I said, and went to open it.

I was pretty sure that we couldn't fix whatever was wrong but decided to let him look. I was rummaging in the trunk for the flashlight when I ended up with my hand in a container of grease.

"Damn," I muttered under my breath while continuing to search.

"What's the matter," he asked, "you fucked up or something?"

My jaw dropped and I stared at him in the dark. I was the one who looked like I had walked out of *Working Woman* magazine.

I calmed down a little and said, "No, just upset."

He looked under the hood, determined that there was nothing we could do, and offered to give me a ride somewhere. I'd remembered seeing a gas station where 238 met highway 17 and figured if I could get there, I could call a friend.

I knew that I should have stayed put and asked him to call for help but instead asked if I could trust him.

He responded with a questioning look and said, "What do you mean?"

"I'm not used to taking rides with strangers," I said.

He shrugged, and I decided to go with him. Remembering my self-defense, I took my keys in one hand and a lit cigarette in the other before I hopped in the car. It didn't take us long to reach the Chevron station.

"Where are you going?" he asked.

"To Hayward." I felt a little more comfortable talking to him now that there was a well-lit gas station in sight.

"I'll take you there if you want," he said.

"Thanks, but I just want to call my friend."

I hopped quickly out of the car, made my call, and was rescued.

I thought about that rumpled biker for a long time. I even considered writing a letter to Ann Landers to thank him properly and to explain why I hadn't been very friendly and hadn't even thanked him.

Journal Guidelines

In your journal entries, try to do as Karen Moody did and follow the guidelines below.

First, try to show the truth: show it as it was or could have been, not as you want to believe it could be. And write without fear of disapproval of others. "You can't find your true voice and peer behind the door and report honestly and clearly to us if your parents are reading over your shoulder. They are probably the ones who told you not to open that door in the first place. You can tell if they're there because a small voice will say, 'Oh, whoops, don't say that, that's a secret,' or 'That's a bad word,' or 'Don't tell anyone you jack off. They'll all start doing it.' . . . Write as if your parents are dead" (Lamott 1994, 198–99).

Second, show people in action: re-create what people said and did. That's the lifeblood of stories. Almost always, showing specifics works better than telling generalities such as "her response upset him," "she waited impatiently," and "Eva was a great kid." Instead of "waited impatiently," show the reader what she *did*: drum her fingernail, tap her foot, light another cigarette, avoid his look, eat another piece of cake, all the above, or what? Specificity. Specificity. Specificity.

In your journal entries, use concrete words instead of abstract or vague ones like *beautiful, nice,* or *brave.* For instance, show your readers how something or someone is "beautiful"—whatever that means; don't just claim that something or someone is beautiful and expect to impress your readers. Use specific words that show what the experiences looked and sounded like. From your writing, readers should be able to see and hear what you had in mind.

To keep your journal entries vivid, severely limit the time and space you re-create. Note, for example, that Karen Moody's journal entry accounts for only an hour or so. The journal entry titled "Annie B. and Oscar Hodges" (reprinted on pp. 23–25) re-creates a short visit: it probably lasts no more than an hour and takes place in and near a rural Tennessee home. Mike Henderson's journal entry (pp. 25–26) covers maybe ten minutes of real time.

Don't tell your readers anything you can show them. Don't, for instance, explain that what you write is funny or sad. Instead, show it in such a way that it *is* funny or sad. One student wrote a journal entry that described a cemetery where adults held each other in grief or stood alone while children ran around and plucked flowers from graves once surrounded by somber adults. Unfortunately, this writer went on to explain what the scene had already shown—that the children stood for life. Such explanations are unnecessary and can alienate readers.

Some other tips about writing journal entries:

1. As you write your journal entries, do not worry about spelling or punctuation. Do not worry about possible errors. Concentrate on putting into words what was said and done or what something looked like and perhaps sounded like. If you eventually use the journal entry, you can correct it later. Besides, worrying about errors as you write is bound to stifle your creativity.

2. Use a separate paragraph for each speaker.

3. Try to show what happened, not impress your readers.

4. It's hard to be precise about the length of a journal entry but, as you will see in the sample journal entries later in this chapter, 1–2 typed single-spaced pages or 2–4 typed double-spaced pages seem to be the usual length.

Types of Writing You Might Include in Your Journal

1. An event that sticks powerfully in your memory. This could be (a) an argument that changed a relationship you had or have, (b) a perplexing experience you suffered through, (c) an experience that led to a surprising conclusion, or (d) an experience that showed you something about people for the first time (for example, that your best friend could betray you)

2. Dialogues that reveal what people are like

3. Outlines or summaries of stories that show how people behave

Another source for journal entries can be annotated postcards. A former student of mine, Lisa Wilson, explained, "When I go to new places, I buy dozens of postcards. I do not mail all of them. Instead, I keep the postcards, and I write about the things that I have seen, heard, or experienced at this place. I write the date and the names of the people that I was with on that particular trip in a corner on the postcard. If there was an interesting comment, observation, or anecdote related to the picture on the postcard, I write that down as well. If at any time my bag becomes crowded with post-cards, I simply start mailing them home to myself."

Do not make entries about what you have done recently or what you are worried about or thinking over. For the reason explained by Ken Macrorie (Macrorie 1980), do not describe recent happenings or your recent thoughts. For now, those will usually prove to be poor sources for stories.

Some writers believe that it's important to jot down what they have to say as soon as possible. Others, such as Woody Allen, say that you will re-member the useful stuff. Still others use a portable tape recorder for at least part of their journals. With those machines, however, you are selecting and recording, not writing.

Remember that, if you like, this journal is for your eyes only, so be can-did about what you write. You may eventually find parts of your journal to be useful in a story, or you may combine parts of the journal to discover a source for a scene or a story. If not, you are at least looking and listening and writing. You are getting—or staying—in shape.

Journal Titles

The following list illustrates the range of possible topics for journal entries:

JOURNAL TITLES BY DEBBIE MINK HOOGE
1. Thanksgiving in Lake Arrowhead
2. The Mink Sisters Singing in Church
3. Baby Heidi
4. Danny Brings Home a Migrant Family
5. Meeting Mama and Vic for the First Time
6. The Red Tennis Shoes
7. Left Behind After the Divorce
8. A Caring Teacher
9. The First Time I Got to Watch Daniel Wrestle
10. Hawaii and Scuba Diving
11. Grandma's Prayer for Death
12. Basketball and Winning
13. Trumpet Solo
14. Annie B. and Oscar Hodges
15. Sixteen
16. Fear at Andrew's Birth
17. Uncle Gus
18. My Sixth-Grade Picture
19. Michael After Six Years
20. Ron and Mom and the Birthday Cakes
21. The News About Kellie
22. Thanksgiving in Mexico
23. Kevin's Homecoming

More Journal Entries

Journal Entry 14: "Annie B. and Oscar Hodges," by Debbie Mink Hooge

We entered their tiny weathered old house from the back porch. The front of the house was fenced off for the comfort of two mean-looking chickens, an old rooster, and a bristled hog. We had to crawl over a broken-down wire fence. My first step into the backyard and my foot was sucked into foul-smelling mud. I looked at my husband. He was standing comfortably on a rock. It was then that I noticed the pathway of stones and bricks that led to the house. Like hopping on stones across a creek, we hopped over the quagmire to the back door. Reaching it, Danny called "Hello . . . hello." Then he pushed the screen door open, and we peered into the dim interior.

It took a moment for my eyes to make the adjustment, but when they did, I saw them. Two ancient people in bibbed overalls sitting in a couple of old rocking chairs gesturing to us. As we stepped inside, I could hear a mumbled, "Hey, Danny, come on in. Ya'll come on in and set down."

To reach them we made our way through the kitchen. At the sink, I noted a hand pump where the faucet should have been. Beneath our feet, the linoleum was peeling and had huge holes worn through. I could see the layers marking the history of the house in the floor. First old wood; a new home at a time when all floors were wood. Then a murky green; maybe it was the first in the hollow. A firehouse red came next, the green worn out by a generation. And last was a washed and dingy yellow; momentary prosperity wiped out by old age. As we neared the doorway into the parlor where they were rocking, I noted the peeling wallpaper and bare and dirty walls. At one spot, you could see sunlight sneaking through.

"Ya'll set down. Set right over there. Good to see you Danny. Good to see you. And, this must be your new wife. Kinda young, ain't she? But purty." I didn't respond since they hadn't spoken directly to me, yet.

"This is Debbie, Annie B. and Oscar." The soft sounding drawl of my husband's voice was a comfort.

Then old Annie B. looked right at me, smiled, said "howdy" and spit into an old coffee can sitting at her feet. She was chewing tobacco! I don't know where the conversation went from that moment. The entire focus of my attention was on that old coffee can, the brown spit that went flying into it, and the old woman who sent it there. Ten rocks of the chair then it came; a steady rhythm and deadly accuracy. She never missed. Occasionally she reached up with her arm and wiped some spittle that had escaped out of the side of her wrinkled and weathered old mouth. The skin where the dribble occasionally appeared was stained a dark brown. On her ancient chin were whiskers. I was mesmerized. I caught snatches of the conversation. "What the hell is a master's degree in chickens going to do you?" "You all need to come home and get a real job down at the factory with your brothers." "California, huh? Kind of wild out there." "I reckon she looks like regular folks. Does she got one of them funny accents?"

Thank goodness for California where sinks had faucets and floors were fixed. Pigs were cartoon characters named Porky, and chickens were plucked and wrapped in cellophane. A land where old ladies smelled like lilacs.

My husband, a native of these hollows of Tennessee, looked comfortable and relaxed talking to these old folks. He was enjoying himself. His Southern accent was restrained and quaint. I found it attractive, but I had never identified him with the South. Four days ago, he had brought me to his home for my first visit. Accepting his family had been easy. Their farmhouse was clean and neat and in verdant surroundings. His family had the same characteristic warmth and graciousness that I found so endearing in my husband. So, when Danny said we needed to go visit Annie B. and Oscar Hodges, I figured it would be fun.

Now, I sat there repulsed and nauseated by the whiskered old woman and her tobacco can with its foaming brown spit. Suddenly Danny stood up. It was time to go. Yes! I stood up and so did Annie B. and Oscar. We said our "nice to meet you" and "good-byes"; then both old folks reached over and gave Danny a hug. Danny stepped away. I turned to follow but didn't make it past Annie B. She gathered me into a great bear hug then brought her head forward. I couldn't believe it. She was going to kiss me. As she bent closer, I could see the dark stains around her mouth and the grizzly gray whiskers. Mesmerized, I almost didn't move fast enough to turn my head so that her kiss landed on my cheek and not my lips. She patted me on the back then spit into her can. "Nice to have met you. You take care of Danny, now, he's a good boy." I managed a faint smile and a choked "Yeah. You, too."

Annie B. and Oscar sat back down in their chairs as we found our own way out of the house. "Ya'll come back, now," they called. Stepping outside the house, I grabbed the tail of my shirt and vigorously rubbed my cheek with it. Through the mud and across the fence, I rubbed. Reaching the car, I heard the strangest choking sound coming from my husband. Finally, the sounds erupted into a full-scale roar of laughter. I wondered if Annie B. and Oscar weren't having a good laugh, too.

"The Convert," by Mike Henderson

Saturday came quickly. I was eating breakfast with my parents when Darrell arrived. As I let him in, I noticed he was fidgeting with a necklace that had an emblem of Christ on the cross.

"Are you Catholic now?" I asked.

"What?" he said.

"The necklace. You've never worn a necklace."

"Are you kidding? I have had this forever," he snapped.

I knew better, and it made me nervous that he had acquired a religious faith only on the day of our journey. As I went to my room to finish getting dressed, I heard Darrell ask my parents if I had told them where we were going and what we were doing. I could hear them from my room.

"Skydiving!" my mom yelled in a disapproving tone. Then she began to laugh, and my father joined her.

"Darrell, you're not a very good liar," my father said.

I joined them in the kitchen as Darrell was trying to convince them that we really were going. They still wouldn't believe him, but there seemed to be a bit of caution in their voices. My father might have known that we were serious because of what he said, "I read in the paper that somebody just died while trying to skydive over there in Lodi," he said. "His chute didn't open or something. I hear that happens a lot."

Darrell looked at me with raised eyebrows, so I quickly said goodbye to my parents and pushed him out the door. As we walked out, I heard my mother call out to us, "Be careful."

We got into my car, and before we were to the end of my street, Darrell began, "Was your dad serious?"

"You know my dad. He was just trying to intimidate us."

"Well, it's working."

"So, you're scared now, huh?"

"Did I say I was scared? Yeah, right. Did I say that? Of course not. It's going to be awesome." There was a slight pause. "But what if it happened? What if our chutes didn't open? What would we do?"

"They have emergency chutes," I said.

"What if they didn't work?" he persisted.

"Then we'd probably die, I guess."

"I don't want to die. I'm too young."

"We aren't going to die. These people know what they are doing, even if we don't. We'll be attached to an instructor. It's not like we'll be by ourselves on our first time."

"But it's always a possibility," he continued.

"I guess so. We can turn around and go back home if you want. I forgot my rosary beads anyway."

"Hell no," he interrupted. "You can go home if you want, but I'm going. Don't wuss out on me now."

Since Darrell seemed to be more confident, I decided to leave well enough alone and not say anything. Besides, now I couldn't keep from thinking about possibilities. I hadn't gotten much sleep the night before either. I had started out thinking of what it was going to be like to jump out of an airplane, but then my mind took control. I imagined myself jumping out in a graceful swan dive and floating through the air like I had seen people do on television, but for some reason I couldn't force myself to picture a good landing. I tried, but, like I said, my mind took over. I would always have trouble opening my chute because I couldn't grab the handle or something. Right before I would hit the ground, the chute would open, but it wouldn't slow me down enough to keep me from slamming into the pavement.

"I'm Getting Married," by Sandi Mendonca

I'm at work at my family's tire business. The familiar yellow car drives in, and I immediately begin to straighten my clothes.

He drives up to the tire machine, gives instructions to the serviceman, and comes into the office. He usually stays outside for a while to talk to the guys.

"Hi," he says as he walks in.

"Hi," I reply, trying to look busy and calm.

As he stands there, he looks awkward, like he has something to tell me. "Did you hear the news?" he asks.

"No, what news?"

"I'm getting married."

I try not to let my emotions show. I've known this for a few days, but it sounds so different coming from him.

"That's good. Congratulations," I say.

We talk for a few minutes by the counter about our other friends who have gotten married and when I will. The serviceman brings in his work order, and I write up the invoice.

We walk outside. He gets into his truck, and we continue to talk. "Do you ever regret anything about us?" I ask.

We look at each other and can see that we regret a lot. I can see by the look in his eyes how he feels about me. I want to tell him how I feel. But I know I shouldn't. It would make it too complicated. But would it help me if I did? Yes . . . and no. Yes . . . and no. That seems to be the answer to all my questions about him.

"Yes and no," he says.

I'm going to miss you. I'll miss our friendship, our long talks on the phone, uptown or on the side of the road. Will you miss me? Do you have to marry her? Does it all have to end? Yes.

We talk for a while longer, neither of us wanting to leave because we know it'll be the last time we talk like this.

"Well, I'd better go," he says.

"Yeah, me too. Thanks for coming in."

"It was nice talking to you," he says, driving away.

"Joe," by Melinda Cornwell

Do I really have to write about Joe? Well, I've put it off for seventeen years. He wasn't the first boyfriend. Worse—the first real love. That thing where your souls, for lack of a better word, jump together like magnets and drag your surprised bodies along with them.

We had study hall. We were two out of thirty who actually studied. Two varieties of the same species—he was a Christian nerd and I was the school-paper kind. Naturally, he invited me to church, a place I enjoyed as much as the dentist. But I went. And went and went. Because afterwards we'd talk.

We could make two cups of coffee at Denny's last longer than any two people in history. Soon we were together all the time. I was experiencing the excruciating mystery of being understood by another person. And a male person at that.

He lived in a tiny house, well back from the road, with his widowed father, a guy as little as his son was tall, who still bore a trace of an Italian accent. Northern Italian, I'd guess, since Joe had an extravagant nose, blond curly hair and the same color eyes as I did—grayblue with that little yellow ring around the pupil. He smelled like poverty—unaired rooms, leftover macaroni, and day-old clothing—with his dad's Old Spice slapped on top.

But I grew to love his guts. And I almost mean his literal guts. At least his narrow chest. His thin but hard white arms. His huge, reddened hands, always cold and damp. The waistband of his boxers. The little holes in his undershirts. I wanted to keep my hands in the back pockets of his highwater corduroys till his friend Jesus came back.

"Great," my friends said. "Does he repent every time you hold hands?"

How little they knew. The limitations on our intimacy increased its eroticism. His mind was innocent, not of sexual facts, but of the consumer images of women held up to adolescent boys. His church forbade TV. He even shunned the annual swimsuit issue. As a result, he wanted me, not some airbrushed image I couldn't possibly replicate. The real, living me, bra size 32A.

But in the end, he said what, given his view of things, he had to say. "I just can't marry an unbeliever." We both cried some, then he said he'd pray for me. I wish I could report that I told him to take his Bible and shove it. But I think I just cried harder.

A year later, I married someone else. Joe went into the military, noncombatant, to get money for seminary school.

Perhaps he still prays for me. I doubt it, though. Meanwhile, I sit and write this confessional, this epistle, this song of songs.

"First Kiss," by Mark Malmberg

It was a Wednesday, and I had just started "going with" an older woman from my church (she was in high school), and I hadn't seen her since Sunday, the day we started going together, and I knew that on this Wednesday night, after the youth group meeting at church, I would be expected to cross that line that could define me as an official teenager: my first real kiss. I had kissed junior high girls before, but it was usually a light peck on the lips. I knew that now that I was dating a real woman I would have to get a little more serious about my kissing technique.

That day at school I was a walking zombie. I had two problems that I had to overcome by that night: (1) how to get her alone and (2) how to apply the kiss.

I tried to figure out the perfect place at church to carry out my plan. How would I get her there? My gut was turning in circles. I played out a zillion scenarios in my head. I practiced conversations with myself, trying to anticipate what she might say to each of my dialogue possibilities.

When I got home from school, I had about three hours to figure things out. I locked myself in the bathroom and began practicing the conversations in front of the mirror, brushing my teeth every five minutes, and practicing "the kiss" on my hand.

I tried to remember every long kiss I had ever seen on television. I tried to remember the way they moved their heads, where they placed their lips, whether the man kissed the upper lip, lower lip, or met both lips straight on. I wondered which way I was supposed to turn my head, how to release the kiss without making a funny noise, and where I was supposed to put my hands.

During the youth meeting, whenever my girlfriend's friends could get me alone, they would ask me, "Are you going to kiss her tonight? She wants you to kiss her. When are you going to kiss her?"

After the meeting, her friends were watching every move we made, and giggling like crazy. They wouldn't leave us alone. I tried some of my dialogue scenarios to get her to the place I planned on kissing her, but they sounded practiced and corny. I felt like an idiot.

Finally, her friends slowly disappeared, and we found ourselves walking nowhere in particular and talking about nothing that either of us was paying attention to.

We stopped, and there was a silence. This was it! My heart was pounding, my palms were sweating, and my mouth was dry as a bone. I didn't know what to say, what to do, or how to do it, but suddenly I was closing my eyes, leaning over, and pursing my lips slightly. Suddenly, as I was anticipating the touching of our lips, my head snapped back and I felt her searching my mouth desperately with her tongue! My eyes were as big as softballs as I tried to get a handle on what was happening. I was only about an inch shorter than she was, but the way she had my head forced back, I felt about a foot shorter than her.

When we finished, my mouth was wet with slobber and I began wiping it with the back of my hand. It hadn't even occurred to me when I was practicing on my hand in the bathroom that this is what would take place. I thought a person had to reach a certain age and maturity before they could start kissing that way. I was expecting to apply a long, passionate kiss with our mouths closed, but I'm glad we didn't! Before my girlfriend and I broke up, a few weeks later, we kissed every chance we had, and I tried to get better with each kiss because I knew there would be more high school girls just around the corner.

Part Two

Studying Stories

Reading is to the mind what exercise is to the body.

—Sir Richard Steele, *The Tatler*

He who has imagination without learning has wings but not feet.

—Chinese Fortune Cookie

3. "Crooked Handlebars"

Allen Lujan

About the Author

The main reason I write is that I believe I have lived an interesting life. By the time I was twenty-two, my mother had been married four times. She always married men who drank and moved around a lot. Between California, Colorado, and Idaho, we moved thirty times. It seems as if I was always the new kid in school. I graduated from high school with a C average, and my worst subject was English; I hated libraries and I hated to read. During my high school years, I read only one book: *The Old Man and the Sea,* by Ernest Hemingway. I would have liked to have read more stories by Hemingway, but I was too afraid to use the library.

My grandfather lived with us for several years and had a lasting influence on me. He was, in my mind, my father. He taught me how to swim and how to throw a curve ball. He drove a blue Volkswagen, smoked Salem cigarettes, and slept with a pillow between his knees. He was a Dodgers fan and a storyteller. He died on my birthday in 1973.

I believe the inspiration for me to write comes not from any talent but from the desire to capture and remember the many people and places that have crossed my life.

Journal Entries 1985–1986

Pappy and Mamo

J Street in Oxnard.
Dogs in backyard.

Antiques everywhere.

Old car in garage (fishing poles, car parts).

Mamo's boxes of jewelry (from swap meets).

Painted his own vehicles.

Grew a "unique" garden.

Flagpole in front yard.

"Kodak" took home movies.

Mamo chewed food in the front of her mouth.

Spanish interpreter (Mamo).

Mamo called us *Mejo*.

Birds that talked—"pretty bird."

Mamo always gave us things (junk), then wanted to know (years later) where they were.

Pappy ate Spanish peanuts, smoked cigars, and drank beer.

Pappy always said: "Eat your green beans and you'll have big feet just like me."

Player piano in the living room.

TV room: big, old, messy bed.

Images from 1981: Pappy

Pappy had a red truck,
he painted it himself.

Always had a garage full of good junk.

Dried out starfish on the roof of his house.

Elk horns in his living room.

Pappy loved to share his Spanish peanuts,
and smoke cigars while he drove his Model A.

Pappy had big feet, always wore dirty white tennis shoes.

Talked to his parakeet in an intelligent way.

Loved his dogs in a brotherly way; fed them with an antique spoon. Taught them how to speak and roll over.

Pappy could drink beer and never get drunk.

Used fish guts for fertilizer in his garden.

Grew turnips the size of pumpkins.

Smoked fish in a barrel cut in half.

Antiques and old bottles in every room,
dog hair on the couch.

"Crooked Handlebars"

As I sat on the bus bench in front of "Marty's Arcade" and watched the traffic go by, my stomach gurgled and churned. I reached up and felt the large bruise on the side of my face. It was still tender. I wondered if Macky, my best friend, believed my story about the two big dudes from the high school.

After a couple of minutes, I saw an old man across the street ride his bike up to the front of "Jue's Liquor." He got off his bike and carefully balanced it on the kickstand. I wasn't sure, but the basket on the front of his bike appeared to hold a bag of groceries. When the man went inside, I stood up and walked across the street.

I approached the bike and looked in the bag. I spotted nothing I particularly liked, except way down at the bottom, underneath the five-pound bag of birdseed and three cans of dog food, I glimpsed a can of Spanish peanuts and a few sticks of jerky. I had never stole a bike before, but I had seen Macky's older brother do it twice. It was no big deal. I climbed on the bike. But right away I had difficulties. The bike was too big, the seat too high, and the bag full of animal food made steering impossible. I rolled about five feet, crushed my balls on the crossbar, and fell to the sidewalk. The three cans of dog food rolled off the sidewalk and into the gutter. I scrambled to get out from under the bike, but my pants leg was hooked on one of the pedals. I kicked and squirmed to get my leg free. Finally, ripping my pants leg, I got free. I slid out from under the army-tank-of-a-bike and rummaged quickly through the bag for the can of peanuts. As soon as I found them and was about to stand up, the man came out of the liquor store. I stood up, looked at the man, and took a step backward. When I saw how big he was, I took another step backward. When he hollered, "You thief!" I decided to run. I turned, tripped over the bike, and fell into the gutter with the dog food.

The man came over, grabbed me by the front of my shirt, and lifted me to my feet. He had big bloodshot eyes and a gray and black stubbly beard. His hair was mostly gray and in a crew cut. As I bent my neck up to look at his face, it seemed to me that he was a giant. I squirmed to get loose, stretching my T-shirt in all directions.

"I was just walking by," I said. "I didn't mean to knock over your bike. It was an accident." The man, possibly thinking that I might crawl out of my T-shirt, put me in a headlock. I finally gave up and just stood there, pinned between the man's arm and his armpit. "It was an accident, Mister. I didn't mean to. Honest." I could smell his strong body odor and cigar smoke.

"Now, if you'll just behave and hold still, I'll think about letting you loose," the man said. As soon as I felt him slacking off with his headlock, I tried to squirm away. But before I could get free, he clamped back down on my head. "You're a stubborn son of a gun, aren't you?" the man said. He held me there for a little while and then slowly let me loose from the headlock. But he didn't let me go. He held me with one of his huge hands by the back of my neck. He turned me toward him and put my face right in front of his. He looked me straight in the eyes. "If it was an accident, why did you try to run?"

"I was scared. You called me a thief." The man slowly let loose of my neck. He smiled.

"You sure looked like a thief to me," he said, as I rubbed the back of my neck. He bent over and picked up his bike. He looked at me, then looked up and down the sidewalk. "I could have sworn that I parked my bike a little closer to the wall." He pointed to a place a few feet up the sidewalk. "I thought for sure I parked my bike right over there."

I looked at the man. He raised his eyebrows and shrugged his shoulders. "I guess it must have rolled a little," he said. "Did you see it roll before it fell over?"

"Yeah. It did roll a little. I tried to catch it, but it was too late." He shook his head.

"Boy, that must have been something," he said. "I wish I could have seen that." I picked up the cans of dog food from the gutter and handed them to the man. He reorganized the bag of groceries, then handed the bag over to me. I hesitated for a second, then I took the bag and looked at the man.

He climbed on his bike and adjusted the basket and the handlebars. They were crooked, and he couldn't get them straight. He got off the bike and tried to straighten the handlebars by holding the front tire between his knees. He grimaced as he tried to force the handlebars back into alignment. They didn't budge, and he gave up.

"How'd you get that bruise on your face?" he asked. "It looks like someone slapped you pretty good."

"I got jumped," I said. "By two guys from the high school."

"Is that right? Did you tell your parents?"

"My mom lives in L.A., and my dad's a longshoreman; he won't be back for a couple of days. But I wouldn't tell them anyway. All I got was this little bruise. I bit the fat guy's ear. The other guy ran away when he heard his buddy screaming. When I stopped biting on his ear, he was crying. He ran away holding on to his ear."

I started to put the bag of groceries back into the basket, but he stuck out his arm to stop me. "I live only a couple of blocks away," he said. "Would you mind carrying that bag home for me? I'd really appreciate the help. It's kind of hard to steer this thing with that big old bag of groceries sitting up front, especially now that my handlebars are a little crooked."

"I should be going," I said.

"It's not far from here," he said. "It will only take a couple of minutes. You don't have to be anywhere, do ya?"

I shook my head. "No," I said. "I'm my own boss. I can go wherever I want."

He got off his bike and started to walk away, pushing the bike beside him. "Come on," he said. "Let's go. I've got to feed a couple of starving dogs."

I felt like setting the bag down on the sidewalk and running off in the opposite direction, but I knew if I did, he'd know for sure that I was a thief. I took a deep breath and followed him. As I caught up to him, I noticed a bottle of liquor sticking out from his back pocket.

I followed behind him for a couple of blocks, wondering where, exactly, we were going. He didn't talk until we turned down an alley.

"I've lived in this neighborhood for thirty years, and this is the first time I've ever had to walk my bike home. I figured it would be a flat tire that would get me, not crooked handlebars." At the end of the alley, we stopped in front of a back gate to a house. He opened the gate. "This is home," he said. "Come on in." He pushed his bike into the backyard. I remained outside the gate, holding the bag of groceries.

"I need to go now," I said, as I bent over to set the groceries next to the gate.

"Nonsense," he said. "Bring that bag on in here. You're in no hurry. You said so yourself."

I stood up straight and remained outside the gate. "Honest, Mister. I got to go."

"My name's Pappy. You don't have to call me *mister*. What's your name?"

"Nick," I said.

"Well, come on in, Nick. I ain't going to bite you." He smiled.

"OK," I said. "But only for a minute."

I stepped past the gate and into the backyard. I held the bag and looked around the backyard while he parked his bike up against the side of the garage. I noticed a large garden, a dirt- and dust-covered boat, a clothesline stretched across a small patch of grass, a bird feeder, a bird bath, a large tree, a covered patio, and a few car parts scattered around. He walked around behind me and closed the gate.

"I don't want my boys to escape," he said, as he walked over to the door leading into the garage. The door was open. He stuck his head into the garage and hollered: "Charlie Brown! Feather! Come here, boys!" He turned and looked at me.

"Not too long ago, a young man jumped my fence and tried to steal the radio off my picnic table. You know what happened?" he asked. I shook my head. "My boys chewed him up a little bit and chased him right back over the fence. These boys have supersensitive sniffers and get real mean when they corner a thief." He stared right at me, but he no longer had a smile on his face.

"Charlie Brown! Feather! Come here, boys." I suddenly had a vision of myself crawling around on the ground while Pappy's dogs chewed me to pieces. I stood still, not knowing what to do or what to expect. I figured I had two choices: confess or run. I quickly ruled out any sort of confession, and as I was about to drop the groceries and make a run for the gate, out of the darkness of the garage emerged two old, scroungy dogs.

Both squinted as they slowly, lazily crept into the backyard. One was a black-and-gray German shepherd, with patches of hair missing from his hind end. The other, a black mutt about the same size as the German shepherd, walked with a limp. Its right front leg was almost useless. The dogs came over to me and began to sniff my shoes and pants legs.

I looked at Pappy. He was smiling. "Don't make a move," he said. "They're liable to attack." I looked at the dogs and shook my head. The dogs continued to sniff my legs. I looked up at Pappy. He broke into loud laughter.

When I realized I wasn't going to be eaten alive, I grinned. "I guess my boys are going to let you off easy," he said. "You're lucky. Come on, bring those groceries into the house. I'm going to fix me a bite to eat. I'll fix enough for the both of us. You look like you could use a good meal."

I took a few steps then stopped. I was hungry, but I didn't know if I could trust Pappy.

"Come on, Nick. You don't want to stay out here. These boys might change their minds about you. But suit yourself. I'm gonna have me some steak and eggs." He turned and started for the back door of his house. I followed behind him with the bag of groceries. Charlie Brown and Feather followed close behind.

The first thing I noticed when I walked in the house was a strong, unfamiliar odor. The second thing I noticed was the dirty pots and pans that filled the sink and covered the stove. On the counter next to the sink, I spotted a large pile of watermelon rinds and a bunch of black moldy bananas. He pushed a bunch of papers out of the way so I could put the bag of groceries on the table.

"One of these days I'm going to finish paying off these bills," Pappy said. "My wife died a couple of weeks ago and now the hospital and the insurance companies are trying to kill me!" I sat down at the table and looked into the living room. The dogs were lying in the middle of the room on the dark brown shag carpet. On the wall, at the far end of the living room, hung a large set of deer horns. Several hats hung from the horns. Beneath the horns stood an upright player piano.

Pappy opened the fridge and looked inside. He pulled out two cans of Coke and handed one to me. He took a dirty glass off the counter and rinsed it out, then reached into his back pocket and pulled out his bottle. It was rum. He poured some in the glass then added some Coke. He took a big drink and looked at me. I took a drink of my Coke and looked into the living room at the dogs. They were looking into the kitchen, watching Pappy.

"I guess I better feed the boys," Pappy said, as he took two cans of dog food from the grocery bag. As soon as Charlie Brown and Feather saw the cans of dog food, they came to the entrance of the kitchen, but no farther. The dogs watched Pappy as he opened the cans. "Mamo, my wife, used to feed these boys. But I was the one who trained them to stop right there on the carpet. They won't come any closer than that, unless I tell them to. Mamo didn't want the dogs under her feet while she was in the kitchen." Pappy took a large spoon from the pile of dirty dishes in the sink. He stuck it into the dog food and looked at the dogs.

"Before Mamo got sick, she took care of these boys just like they were her own kids. Now look at them. They're not as happy as they used to be. I think they expect her to come back. For all they know, she's just on a vacation. I don't know. What do you think, Nick?" Pappy took another drink of his Coke and rum.

"I don't know," I said. "Maybe. But, I've never had a dog."

"I don't know either, Nick, and I've been around dogs all my life." Pappy took another drink and motioned for the dogs to come into the kitchen. They both came in and sat down in front of him. Pappy dug out a heaping spoonful of dog food from one of the cans and held it out for Charlie Brown to eat off the spoon. He did the same thing for Feather. After the cans were empty and the spoon licked clean by Charlie Brown, Pappy let the dogs out into the backyard. He took a big drink and emptied his glass. "Why don't you go wash up in the bathroom, Nick? It's right around the corner and to your right. I'll start us something to eat." I stood up and walked out of the kitchen.

In the short hallway leading to the bathroom, I stopped to look at some pictures hanging on the wall. In several of them, I could pick out Pappy when he was younger. His wife appeared to be a beautiful woman with big brown eyes and wavy brown hair. I looked at all the photos, and in all of them, Mamo and Pappy were happy and smiling, dancing or fishing or bowling. One photo showed Mamo hugging Pappy from behind, while Pappy, with a big smile on his face, held up a big fish.

At the end of the hallway, across from the bathroom, I stopped and looked into a bedroom. The curtains were pulled back, and light filled the room. In the middle of the room, without any sheets or blankets, was a bed that looked like it belonged in a hospital; it had side rails and sat high off the floor. On one side of the bed was a wheelchair and a walker. In the wheelchair, three pillows without slips sat stacked one on top of the other. On the other side of the bed stood two TV trays. One held a water pitcher and several plastic cups, all empty and turned upside down. The other tray contained several plastic prescription bottles—still with pills in them—and a Bible. The dresser at the foot of the bed was covered with get-well cards and small framed photos. On the walls of the room, hung in no particular order, I noticed framed photos of antique cars. There was a strong odor to the room, one that I had never smelled before.

I walked into the bathroom and smelled the same odor, but it wasn't as strong. There was a cushioned white seat in the bathtub with a towel draped over the backrest. I looked in the mirror and could see the outline of my father's fingers on my face. I touched the bruise with the tips of my fingers. Just above my right cheek, it was still tender and almost looked like I had a black eye. I looked at my T-shirt. It was stretched out in front, mostly around the neckline. I washed my hands and face and dried them on a towel that hung on the back of the bathroom door. The towel was brown and had an antique car printed on it. That's when I noticed the wallpaper: more antique cars, printed over and over. Before I left the bathroom, I looked one more time in the mirror, turning my face from side to side, wondering how long it would take for the bruise to go away.

When I walked back into the kitchen, I noticed that Pappy had refilled his glass. I sat down. Pappy stood in front of the stove.

"How's scrambled eggs sound, Nick?"

"Sounds good," I said. "I like eggs."

Pappy handed me a plate heaped with scrambled eggs, cut-up weenies, and a couple of flour tortillas. He sat down at the table, and we started to eat. "Where do you live? Around here?"

"I live at the far end of Thompson Boulevard, across from the fairgrounds."

"You know, Nick, my wife used to love to go to the fair. She liked to go at nighttime when the sky was all lit up from the Ferris wheel. She mostly liked to just walk around and watch all the people. We'd spend a few bucks pitching dimes, but mostly we just walked around. Sometimes we'd stop and buy a corn dog from one of the concession stands." Pappy finished his eggs and weenies and leaned back in his chair. I continued to eat. He took a drink from his glass. His eyes were still red, and he looked tired. He scratched his beard and stared out the window across the kitchen table. "She was a good woman, Nick. I don't think a better wife or woman ever lived. I certainly didn't deserve her. Her heart was much bigger than mine." For the first time, he had a sad look. He stared out the window and continued to talk.

"I should have never let her go back to the hospital. She wanted to die in her own bed, in her own house. But Nick, I just couldn't handle it. I had to get up at all hours of the night, night after night, and give her pain medication. Sometimes she'd wake me up and beg me for more medication, not knowing that I had just given her some only a few minutes earlier. She lost her hair and went blind, right before my eyes. It was killing me. I felt I had no choice but to put her in the hospital. It was the hardest thing I ever had to do. Two days after I admitted her, she passed away. I should have let her die here, Nick, but I was falling apart. I wasn't doing her any good. I started to have bad feelings about her."

He took a drink, then sat his empty glass on the table. "I don't know why I'm telling you all this. You probably think Pappy's some babbling old fool." He looked at me and smiled. "Come here, Nick. I want to show you something." I stood up and followed Pappy out the door and into the backyard. We walked past the dogs, lying on the sidewalk in the late afternoon sun, and over to the open garage door. He walked into the garage and turned on the light. There was a large car, covered with a couple of old paint tarps. Pappy walked over to the front of the garage and opened the big garage door.

"This was Mamo's baby. We bought this old boy back in '59. I painted it, and Mamo did the upholstery." Pappy walked over to what looked like the front of the car and motioned for me to come over. "Grab that tarp and fold it back, like this." We folded back the tarps and exposed the dark, shiny, midnight-blue car. "This is what you call a Model-A," Pappy said. He walked over to a counter and picked up a half-smoked cigar. He lit it and took a couple of puffs. He reached above the counter and took a driving cap off a shelf. He shook off the dust and put the cap on his head. He walked to the front of the car, opened the hood, connected the battery cable to the battery, and closed the hood. Pappy looked at me and took a puff off the cigar. "You want to go for a ride in a Model-A?"

"Sure," I said. "I've never been in one before."

"Well, good. This will be fun. I'll tell you what, we can kill two birds with one stone. I need to go visit Mamo at the cemetery, and I suppose you could use a ride home. It's going to be getting dark in a little while; I'd hate for you to get jumped again. That's a long walk over to the fairgrounds."

"I walk home all the time," I said. "I'm not afraid. But if you want to give me a ride home, it's all right with me."

Pappy smiled and adjusted his hat. We both got in the car and closed the doors. The car smelled old and musty, but I liked the smell. Pappy tapped the gas pedal with his foot and pushed a button next to the steering column. The engine made a slow, grinding, wheezing noise then started with an abrupt shake. Pappy looked at me and grinned. I grinned back. I felt like I was about to leave on a grand adventure.

"Here we go," Pappy said. He put the car in gear, and we lunged forward. As we exited the darkness of the garage, the car shone brightly. Pappy got out, closed the garage door, kicked a rear tire, then got back inside. As we started down the alley, Pappy reached under the dash and sounded an ooga horn.

By the time we arrived at the cemetery, the sun was starting to go down. I stood outside the car while Pappy walked over to Mamo's fresh gravesite. The cemetery was empty. A few gravesites had flowers in front of the headstones, but mostly the headstones were starting to get overgrown with grass and weeds. Mamo's grave, under a large oak tree, still had flowers placed around the headstone. Pappy stood in front of the grave with his hat off. He stared down at the headstone. Every once in a while he would look away, at the sky or the other end of the cemetery. After about ten minutes, Pappy slowly made his way back to the Model-A. I couldn't tell for sure, but I think he had been crying. We got back in the Model-A and slowly drove out of the cemetery.

Pappy began to smile again when we turned onto Main Street. He hit the ooga horn when someone waved from a passing car. People stared at us as we made our way down Main Street. The old car received quite a bit of attention, which I liked. People stopped on the sidewalks and watched as we rattled down the street. All the streetlights were on, and the Model-A shined and glistened. Pappy lit his cigar again and blew smoke rings. The sweet smell filled the car.

Pappy crossed the railroad tracks and turned down Thompson Boulevard. Two blocks later I pointed out my house and Pappy pulled over to the curb. It was almost dark.

"Listen, Nick. I really appreciate you carrying that bag of groceries home for me today. I don't know what I would have done without you. You're a good kid. I enjoyed your company. I'm sorry I called you a thief. I realize now that you couldn't have been trying to steal my bike. You're too smart for that. Nobody as smart as you would've ever tried to ride a bike as big as mine." I smiled and nodded my head in agreement. "And, Nick, I'd like to let you know that if you ever need any help, with anything, you know where I live. I have a feeling that whoever hit you in the face isn't going to go away. They're probably just as tough as you are. I know you can take care of yourself but—just in case, I want you to know you can always come see me."

I looked Pappy in the face. "I'm OK. I can handle it."

"I know. I'm just letting you know."

"Thanks," I said, and opened the door. I stepped out onto the curb and closed the door.

Pappy reached over and rolled down the window. "Say, listen, Nick. I'm going to take the boat up to Lake Casitas tomorrow and do a little fishing. You're welcome to come along. I heard the bass are hitting pretty good. Do you know how to fish?"

"Yeah. A little. Not too good."

"I can give you some tips. I'm sort of rusty, myself. How 'bout it. You want to go for a boat ride?"

I smiled. "Sure. I'll go."

"I'll pick you up right here, in the morning, say around eight o'clock. OK?"

"OK, Pappy. I'll be here." He revved the engine, and I turned to walk away. The Model-A rolled a few feet forward then I heard a squeak from the brakes. I turned back around.

"Oh, Nick. One more thing." I walked over near the curb. I could see Pappy smiling. Over the rattle of the Model-A he said: "If you're ever out shopping for a bike, I recommend you check to see how big it is before you give it a test ride. Just a word of advice." He waved. I smiled and waved back. He revved up the engine and started down the street. I stood on the curb and watched. Across from the fairgrounds, the red taillights faded from view.

Interview

1. *Approximately what percentage of "Crooked Handlebars" is factual (happened to you or others)?*

It's hard to say, but maybe 75 to 80 percent of "Crooked Handlebars" is factual. Pappy is my step-grandfather and resides today in Moro Bay. Mamo was my step-grandmother and did die from cancer in 1983. I recall that the slow progression of her cancer (and death) were hard times for Pappy. He did, in fact, resort to the use of hard liquor to cope with Mamo's passing. Pappy the character is drawn exactly from my view of Pappy the person. The same is true of the backyard, garage, kitchen, and bathroom in "Crooked Handlebars"; these descriptions come directly from my memory and photographs.

2. *About what percentage of the events in your story is* your *experience?*

In a sense, I'm the boy in "Crooked Handlebars." Nick's observations of Pappy and Pappy's house are my own observations. I had visited Mamo and Pappy before Mamo's death; Mamo's bones were so brittle she couldn't get out of bed; she was blind and confused (due to the morphine). Pappy was gaunt and drank rum and Coke to cope with the situation.

I also visited the house after Mamo passed away. This visit remains clear in my mind. Mamo's absence was overwhelming. It was this visit that becomes Nick's experience in "Crooked Handlebars." I can still recall stopping at Mamo's bedroom door and peering in. She was gone, but her death lingered.

3. *About how many short stories had you written before you wrote "Crooked Handlebars"?*

Before "Crooked Handlebars" I had written five other short stories. I must say that I struggled greatly while writing these stories. It was not fun, and it was not easy. Writing fiction was (and still is) very time-consuming for me; I'd spend hours on just one paragraph, only to throw it away in the end.

4. *How did you plan your story?*

Originally, the story got out of control. I had too much happening, too many scenes, and no real conflict or resolution. After a conference with Dr. Phillips, it was clear that I needed to make the conflict between Nick and Pappy more defined. I needed to show that both characters were in need of each other. Establishing their friendship became the conflict. Could they become friends? Were they compatible? Could the teacher (Pappy) teach the student? Could the young boy find sympathy and respect for an older struggling man? When the conflict became clear, it was just a matter of finding the right time to close the story.

5. and 6. *What were the major steps you went through in writing and rewriting "Crooked Handlebars"? In rewriting your story, what helped you the most?*

I like to start by writing everything out in pencil: ideas, brainstorms, and rough drafts. After I get a good start on a rough draft (4–6 single-space pages), I plug it into the computer. The next day I print a copy of the rough draft and take a close look at it. At this point the fun begins. I start adding new paragraphs, and the story begins to grow rapidly. After each session at the computer, I print a copy to see how long the story is and to find out where more detail is needed. I also look in my journals for something that might fit into the story. It seems there's always something in my journals that will add to a story—probably because most of my stories begin as journal entries.

Persistence and time (letting the story rest) have always helped me with rewriting. In between rewrites, I always get new ideas and a clearer picture of where the story "might" be going.

For one reader's feedback about "Crooked Handlebars," see pp. 120–23 (chapter 9).

4. "Treason and Vengeance"

Rosa M. Díaz

About the Author

By age twelve writing had become a very personal way to communicate what I couldn't say orally. I grew up in Central California and attended California State University, Stanislaus, where I earned a BA in Spanish with a minor in Chicano Studies and where I discovered my special interest and career as a writer. I wrote several short stories and some short film scripts. My treatment for a short screenplay was published in the first edition of *Writing Short Scripts,* and the complete script was reprinted in the second edition of that book. Some of my writings were published by university publications, and several of my poems have been included in poetry anthologies.

I remember listening to my parents tell stories about their relatives, stories that captured my attention. I felt I knew those people. I even felt I'd been in places that my parents talked about. For me, writing is a way to become eternal and, like memories that are recounted, writing calls forth a lot of emotions. I began a journal in 1990. Writing, then reading, about past actions and feelings makes me see the mistakes I made and, at the same time, helps me learn from my own experiences. I hope many people can also learn from my life experiences.

"Treason and Vengeance"

I

Gabriella comes to the sofa and sits next to Charles. She caresses his face and plays with his curly hair. She looks at him for an instant and sighs; then she cuddles up on his bare and hairy chest. Gabriella puts Charles's arms around her. He watches TV.

Gabriella asks, "Charles do you love me?"

Charles doesn't respond. Gabriella hugs him tighter, but suddenly she sits up. "You won't believe what happened. One of my niece's friends is pregnant! She's only fourteen and already pregnant. I cannot believe it." Gabriella waits for his reaction. She speaks louder, "Ashley said that her friend is going to have an abortion because her parents don't know about her pregnancy. Can you believe it? I thought that these things only happened in the big cities."

Gabriella looks at Charles. She stands up. "Tsah! You don't care anyway!" she says, straightening her white summer dress, and walks to the kitchen.

Gabriella puts some water on to boil with some tea bags. Charles walks into the kitchen and sees Gabriella slam the pot down on the stove. Her big brown eyes seem slanted, and her face looks tense. He walks up to her and tries to embrace her.

"I'm sorry. What were you saying?"

Gabriella pushes his arms away. "No. I'm not repeating myself. You had your chance."

"Come on. I was watching the news. Tell me, what happened?"

Gabriella walks by Charles to the refrigerator and opens the icebox, but she doesn't know what to get and closes it again. Charles waits. She's quiet, then, through the bangs around her face, looks at him out of the corner of her eye. "Don't worry. It's nothing important! Go watch your stupid show," Gabriella mumbles under her breath.

Charles picks up his shirt from the chair and puts it on. He looks at Gabriella, but she doesn't say anything. Charles turns to the television set. He sees the commercials are over and walks back to the sofa. With the remote control, he turns up the volume. Gabriella turns the air conditioner off and opens the kitchen curtains and window. She feels the warmth of the evening on her face, and she's momentarily breathless. She walks back to the counter and leans on it. Folding her arms, she looks at the tea boiling.

II

Gabriella is replanting flowers in the backyard. She hears the doorbell ring several times and runs inside to see who it is. Before she opens the door, she takes the gardening gloves off and checks herself in the oval brass mirror by the door. Gabriella takes the cloth gloves off and runs her fingers through her shiny hair. Then she picks a red lipstick from the plant stand to retouch her lips and opens the door.

"Oh Fabián. What a surprise." Gabriella and Fabián warmly embrace. Fabián gently moves back and Gabriella kisses him on the face, close to the lips. "*¿Cómo estás?*" she whispers.

"Fine," Fabián answers and walks inside. He passes by the mirror and notices the lipstick mark on his face. He tries to clean it with his hand but smears it. Gabriella shyly looks away.

"Sit down. What brings you here?"

"Oh, I just wanted to see how you were doing."

"Mm. How nice of you." Fabián lowers his head and turns it aside. Gabriella sits on the other end of the sofa. "What's wrong?" Fabián raises his head, and Gabriella notices his eyes are watery. "Is it your girlfriend, again?" she asks. She folds one leg and puts it on the sofa and leans against the back of the sofa, placing her arm on the back edge. She faces Fabián.

Fabián gets in a similar position as Gabriella's. "Well, she treats me like a toy. She calls me only when she needs something from me."

"And whose fault is it?"

"Maybe it's mine. But I can't help it. I like her a lot."

"Yeah. But I don't think she wants to be with you."

"The thing that hurts me most is that she doesn't take my calls."

"What a dumb girl."

"What should I do?"

"Make her miss you. Don't take her calls and don't call her either."

"It's going to be hard."

"I also have some problems of my own."

"Really, what's wrong?"

"I've been feeling very nervous. My work is piling up. It seems every-thing comes at once."

"Oh Gabriella, that's nothing compared to what I've been going through. I cannot get in the credential program. I have to work two jobs to support myself. My car broke, and I couldn't get a ride. And to top it off, this girl treats me like . . ."

"Like garbage," says Gabriella. Fabián nods. "Well, your problems seem great to you. My problems seem great to me," she says, looking straight into Fabián's small eyes.

A moment later, Gabriella gets up and brings back two glasses with soda. Fabián looks at himself in the mirror above the sofa. He tries to take the smeared lipstick off with his hand. Gabriella leaves the tray on the coffee table and brings a wet napkin.

"I'm sorry. Here. This will take it off," she says in a soft voice.

"What is it?"

"It's just some lotion. Let me do it for you."

Fabián and Gabriella sit on the sofa. He moves closer and leans to-ward her. Gabriella gets the napkin from his hand and holds his face with one hand. She spreads her lean fingers on his chin and is able to feel his pulse beat rapidly. He looks down, avoiding her eyes.

III

Gabriella and Charles sit in the backyard. "October is a weird month. One day is hot, the next one is cold," she says as she goes inside to turn the radio on. She searches for the music.

"Leave it there. I like rock!" Charles hollers.

"That's better!"

"Oldies?! You're like an old lady!"

Gabriella returns to the backyard. "With the new kind of music, no one can think. No wonder there's so many ignorant kids nowadays."

"You're so old-fashioned!"

"No. I have taste. With this music I can think and concentrate. I don't have headaches, and I don't have to shout at you."

"OK, OK!"

Gabriella picks up her book, but the bright afternoon sun doesn't let her read. "Oh, I'm not in the mood for studying." Gabriella slams the book closed. "Do you have a lot to study?" Charles shakes his head.

Gabriella sits on Charles's lap and tries to kiss him on the lips. He contorts his mouth to the opposite side. She tries to kiss him on the face, but he lowers his head and keeps reading. She kisses his neck, but he shudders and puts his head in the way. "Leave me alone! I'm trying to read!"

Gabriella stands up. "If you don't want my kisses, some other guy will!"

"I'm sorry."

"No, you're not. You're always rejecting me. I'm getting tired of it. If you lose me, you lose the best!"

"I'm sorry!"

"Don't be, just don't do it."

"It's just that I have to read."

"You could say that, but don't reject me because other guys would give anything for one of my kisses."

"Why should I get wet for nothing?"

"Yeah, I forget you're ready for sex, not for affection." Some tears show in Gabriella's eyes. She picks up her reading glasses and her book and walks inside. "Lock the door when you leave. I'm going to take a shower."

Gabriella lets herself fall on the bed. She can hear Charles slam the patio door shut and start the car, squealing the tires as he drives away.

IV

The music resounds throughout Gabriella's house. The doorbell rings, and she tries to stand up from the sofa, but she weakens and falls on the edge. "I'm coming!" she says in a rough voice. She leaves the champagne glass on the coffee table and, struggling, stands up. She opens the door and closes her eyes a little, focusing on the visitor.

"Hi Gabriella," says Fabián. Gabriella smiles at him and pushes the door open. She's about to lose her balance, but Fabián is quick to hold her up.

"Oops!" Gabriella says as she surrenders.

Fabián picks her up and carries her to the sofa. Gently he makes Gabriella lie down, but then she sits up. Fabián picks up the glass and tastes the champagne left. "You're getting drunk on champagne?"

"Yeah. Any—" she burps, "anything gets to me."

Fabián lowers the volume. "What made you get drunk? What makes you listen to this depressing music?"

"It's not depressing. It's romantic."

"In your condition and—"

"Put it louder! Air Supply's music makes me cry every time," she slurs out her words.

"You don't need to cry."

"Yes, I do!"

The record is over. Fabián turns it to the other side and turns the volume just a little bit higher. "Tell me, what got you this upset?"

"Nothing!"

"Nothing?" Fabián kneels at Gabriella's feet and dries her tears with his handkerchief.

"I just feel rejected. Charles ignores me."

"Oh, don't worry. He'll come to his senses."

"He doesn't listen to me, and he rejects my affection."

"Maybe he has some other problems."

"Maybe it's me. I'm ugly. I'm stupid. I'm boring," she says covering her face with her hands.

"No, you're not ugly. In fact, I think you're very beautiful and sexy, too. Plus, you're very smart."

"You really think so?" she says slowly taking her hands off her face.

"Yeah. You're very logical in your thinking. I'm always asking you for advice, aren't I?"

"No. I mean about me being beautiful."

"Yes. You are. I've always thought you were beautiful, inside and out."

"How come you never told me?"

Fabián clears his throat. "Let me fix you some coffee. Where do you keep all that stuff?" He stands up and waits for her answer.

Gabriella reaches out for his hand. "Stay here, please. I feel everything going in circles."

"Of course. You almost finished the whole bottle." Fabián makes Gabriella lie down on the sofa. He brings some pillows and blankets from her bedroom. He takes her shoes and sweater off and covers her with the blankets. Fabián fixes the pillows under her head and drinks the rest of the champagne.

"It hurts that Charles doesn't want my kisses," Gabriella mumbles.

Fabián sits on the edge of the coffee table. "If he doesn't, I do," Fabián says, as he kisses her face. She smiles and falls asleep. Fabián brushes Gabriella's long black wavy hair to the back, and it hangs over the pillow and the armrest. He stays there, watching her sleep, caressing her face.

v

In the dining room, Gabriella sets the table for two and takes the fine china and crystal glasses from the hutch. Then she places the napkins and lights the candle. She turns the lights off and smiles, satisfied at the sight. *Perfecto,* she thinks. He's a little late, but that's OK. Gabriella looks at her watch. She goes into the bedroom and opens the jewelry chest. She looks through the jewelry, deciding which gold earrings to wear.

"Gabriella!" Charles says as he opens the front door. "Gabriella!"

Gabriella comes rushing into the living room. "You startled me." She raises her arms to embrace him. "Charles, were you drinking? You stink like cheap alcohol."

"I just had a couple of beers with my family."

"No wonder!"

Charles picks Gabriella up and kisses her desperately. Gabriella punches him on the chest violently. Charles carries her to the bedroom, and together they fall on the bed. Gabriella kicks and punches Charles's big muscular body and finally manages to get away. She stands up abruptly.

"It's easy for you to come here and get whatever you want out of me. But no more!" She walks back and forth. Charles lies on the bed. "You're ready to have sex but never to make love. Well, not me! I am a woman, and I want affection, not the sexual act!" Charles turns on his back and covers his face with his arms. Gabriella rushes to the front door and opens it. "Get out! Get out now before I call the police!"

Charles walks to the kitchen slowly. He gets a pot and fills it with water. He puts it on the burner and searches for something in the cabinet. "Just let me make a cup of coffee so I can drive back."

"How did you get over here, huh?!"

"Give me some time so I can get sober again."

"Did I tell you to drive in your condition? Get out!" Gabriella says, still holding the door open.

Charles stays next to the stove, waiting for the water to boil. "I'm sorry," Charles mumbles.

Gabriella closes the door and sits at the table in the kitchen. "I want romance and affection. I want passion and seduction. I dream of a man who makes me tingle. I prefer a thousand kisses for one sex act. I want so many things, but you offer me so little!"

"You watch too many soap operas."

"And you watch too many killer movies!"

Charles prepares the coffee in a Styrofoam cup. He puts everything away and smiles at Gabriella, waiting for her approval, but she doesn't respond. She stares at the candle burning in the dining room and sighs. He walks to the door and holds it open. "Bye," he whispers.

Gabriella follows Charles to the door. "Bye," she answers, with a smile.

Charles walks out, and Gabriella slowly closes the door behind him.

VI

Gabriella and Fabián are waiting for the movie to begin. It's a cold starry night. Fabián turns the heater on. The car soon warms up, but the windows get foggy. Gabriella takes her coat off, and Fabián cleans the front window. Fabián leans back and discretely looks at Gabriella as she tosses her long hair back. She reaches for her purse on the floor and places it between her and the door.

Gabriella clears her throat. "You want a kiss?" Gabriella asks and smiles. Fabián looks straight into her sparkling eyes. She opens her hand and offers him a Hershey's Kiss.

In the darkness, Fabián sees the candy in Gabriella's hand. "Oh!" he says, taking the chocolate from Gabriella. He puts it in his mouth, avoiding direct eye contact.

"Were you expecting the other kind?" she asks.

He looks down.

"If you want, I give it to you."

After a while Gabriella looks intensely through the window. Fabián covers her face with kisses and caresses. "Fabián, we should stop."

"You don't like it? You don't want to do it?"

"God knows I do! But I am betraying Charles."

"It's his fault. If he only gave you what you ask for."

"But still it's not right."

"Are you satisfied with what he gives you?"

"*Bueno, no pero—*"

"You trapped me in your flirtatious and seductive game and now . . ."

"But?"

"Just relax. Let things happen if they are going to happen."

"Hold me and kiss me all you want, but nothing more. Please."

"Shh," Fabián whispers in Gabriella's ear and covers her face with kisses and caresses. She breathes deeply, closes her eyes, and offers him her lips. The tangled bodies slide down on the car seat.

VII

The next evening, Gabriella comes into her house. It's dark; she turns the lights on and sees Charles sitting in the chair next to the lamp. As he taps the armchair with his fingertips, Gabriella is startled.

"Where were you?" he asks, clenching his teeth.

"Don't ever do that again! You scared the heck out of me!"

"Where were you?" Charles says.

"Where were you? I was waiting all day for you," Gabriella says.

Charles stands up and holds Gabriella by the hair. He grips her hair and pulls downward. She looks at him straight in the eye, breathing hard. "Somebody told me that you went out on me."

"I was with Fabián, but that doesn't mean I went out on you."

"What did you guys do?"

"We went to the park, but we didn't do anything bad."

"What are you hiding from me, Gabriella?"

"Nothing! He just wanted to talk to me. He's my friend."

"I don't believe in friendship between men and women."

"That's your problem. But I'm telling you the truth. He wanted my advice."

"Really? He should get a psychologist instead. What's his phone number? I want to make sure."

"You're crazy!"

"If you have nothing to hide, let me call." Charles pulls harder on Gabriella's hair; then he lets it go suddenly and her head bounces forward.

Gabriella dials the phone. It rings many times. Finally there's an answer. "Hello, Fabián?"

Charles snatches the mouthpiece from Gabriella. "Fabián, where did you and Gabriella go last night?"

Gabriella lies down on the beige rug. She lies with her back towards Charles and stares through the French doors. She covers her ears with her arms, but Charles's questioning and shouting echo in her eardrums. Charles is quiet for a moment; then Gabriella hears him say, "I have given everything to make Gabriella happy. Don't you see she used you to make me jealous?" Gabriella slowly sits up but doesn't say anything.

"You want me to tell her that? OK," Charles says and hangs up the phone.

Charles goes into the bedroom and takes the jewelry he has given Gabriella through the years. He looks through the hallway closets and takes the fur coat he gave her one Christmas. She lies back down on the floor.

Charles speaks to Gabriella as he looks throughout the house. "Your 'friend,' Fabián López, said that he doesn't want to see you ever again. He doesn't want to be used by you anymore. He says that he doesn't want to interfere in our problems. But, fortunately, there's nothing more between us." He pauses as he closes a closet door and continues, "You know, it hurts me more because Fabián used to be my friend, too. I always thought you had good principles, but I was wrong! And you say you're the best one for me? Ha! You're worth nothing!"

Charles puts the jewelry in his shirt pocket. He takes his key chain out, pulls a key out, and throws it to Gabriella. As Charles walks to the door, he arranges the fur coat on his arm. He slams the door behind him. The light bulb in the living room burns out, and the house is dark and quiet. Gabriella lies on the floor with her eyes wide open. The moonlight illuminates her motionless silhouette.

Interview

1. *Approximately what percentage of "Treason and Vengeance" is factual (happened to you or others)?*

About 85 percent of the story is true.

2. *About what percentage of the events in your story is your experience?*

Of my own experience, the story contains 85 percent.

3. *About how many short stories had you written before you wrote "Treason and Vengeance"?*

I had written one or two.

4. *How did you plan your story?*

I looked back in my life and thought that if I wrote what happened at one point of my life, I could perhaps find my mistakes or those of others and try to learn and change from those mistakes.

5. *What were the major steps you went through in writing and rewriting your story?*

From my own experiences, I wrote about what had happened and when. Although I mixed some of the dates and situations, it pretty much happened as it did. But in real life this situation went on for over one year. And encounters with Fabián were only two, and nothing major happened between Gabriella and Fabián.

6. *In rewriting your story, what helped you the most?*

It helped me the most to put everything in perspective from a third person. And for dramatic purposes, I changed the sequence of events. Also, the group feedback was useful.

5. "Intruders"

Claire Doud

About the Author

I was born the eldest of ten. My parents gave us a loving and stable home. They honored God and were devoted to one another. For as long as I can remember, I've possessed the mixed blessing of an introspective mind. Although I thrived on the commotion and constant activity of a large family, I'd often retreat to quiet lonely places to read, write, or think.

At age twenty I entered the Vista program, which changed my life in more ways than one, for there I met my husband while serving in Oklahoma. However, the physical and spiritual poverty I saw there repulsed and depressed me. The security blanket of my youth began unraveling. Although I was disenchanted with the program, my Vista experiences expanded my horizons and fostered a sense of social consciousness and commitment.

For years I've struggled with illnesses and other seemingly insurmountable challenges. Although some were like sieges that lasted longer than I care to remember, the struggles have helped me add depth to my writing. Yet, despite these painful challenges, I've retained a belief that God has a sure hold on my life.

Presently I teach Language Arts and Yearbook to eighth graders in a fairly rural district not far from my home. Oddly enough, my students come from homes quite similar to those of my early Vista days.

▷ "Intruders"

"Morning, Joanie. Had breakfast yet?" Mom sat down next to me and gave my hand a big squeeze. Dad took my other hand in his and offered a word of prayer. I closed my eyes and felt the warm sun on my face. The delicious scent of sweet william filled the morning air. Life had returned to normal.

It was then that the phone rang, punctuating Dad's quiet moment of thanksgiving. I bounded out of my chair and ran toward the hallway, hoping that Paul was calling to ask me out. "Hello," I answered with a light, expectant spring in my voice.

"I have a collect call from Kim Ackerman. Will you accept the charges?"

Calling collect! Kim had a lot of nerve. "Yes," I quietly told the operator.

Kim had driven me to the airport in Oklahoma City, just three and one half months ago, in the middle of the biggest thunderstorm of my life. We'd shared a duplex together when we were Vista Volunteers in Tulsa, until Rodney drifted into her life and she'd lost all sense of time, friendship, and responsibility. I hadn't forgiven her, and our parting words had been cool.

I wondered what she could be calling me about. I'd heard through other Vistas that she'd married Rodney and moved back to Brooklyn. But things hadn't gone well for her there. It seemed that the Brooklyn relatives weren't any more accepting of Rodney's black skin than his family had been of their mixed marriage. I felt as if I should feel sorry for them, but I didn't. I never wanted to see them again.

"Joanie, I'm so glad you were home." There was a hesitant catch in her shaky voice.

"What's wrong, Kim? Are you all right?" I asked, more out of a sense of decency than concern.

"James is dead, Joanie. They shot and killed him! The police shot and killed him in his own kitchen!"

"When? Why?" I mumbled. My stomach knotted up as I experienced confusion, then rage as Kim related the details. Waves of nausea overwhelmed me as she described the pool of blood that his wife and daughter had to mop up afterwards. I felt as if I were going to throw up.

"It happened just yesterday afternoon," she continued, "I called you just as soon as I could. I thought you'd want to know."

I wanted to scream at her to stop. Instead, I kept my voice even. "Oh, yes, Kim, I'm so glad you called."

It had taken me three whole months to feel somewhat normal again. I wanted to forget the whole bizarre experience. I wanted to forget those nine months and file them away, forever. I'd already put it all behind me. Now she was calling and undoing everything.

"If it had been a white man, it wouldn't have happened," Kim persisted. "I just don't understand people," she sobbed into the phone. "Couldn't they just have shot him in the leg or something?"

"I don't know," I answered weakly. I desperately wanted out of the conversation and was still struggling with waves of nausea.

I remembered Mom and Dad and hoped they weren't waiting breakfast for me. I pulled the cord around the corner, set the phone on the kitchen table, and called toward the patio, "It's long distance." They nodded at me through the window. I sank down in one of Mom's fluffy cushions and eased my now aching back against the wide wooden slats while Kim rattled on. I stared at the porcelain vase. Mom's freshly cut roses fluttered in the early morning breeze that came from the open window above the sink, and I thought about life being so fragile.

Kim told me that Rodney still wasn't working, but that he was thinking about going back to school. Then she added, "We don't do drugs any more either."

"Oh," was all I could say. I'd begun to feel light-headed and shivered as my body got very cold—then hot—all over.

"I've got to go," I interrupted, "I think I'm going to be sick."

She sounded surprised. "Oh, OK," then quickly added, "Rodney and I have been thinking about moving out to California. We'll look you up."

"Sure," I muttered, but thought, don't you dare!

I pulled myself slowly out of the chair. I didn't think I would make it to the bathroom in time, so I leaned over the kitchen sink and took deep breaths. The nausea began to subside. Before returning to the kitchen table, I filled a glass with water and took a long swallow. My head was pounding, so I pressed my temple hard against the butcher block. Then, the old smells came back to me. They filled my nostrils and forced me to remember: the fried okra, the barbecued ribs, the ever-present mildew. They wouldn't let me escape.

I tried to get the image out of my mind: James lying there beneath the pink Formica table, with two bullet holes in his chest and two more in his head, one of them in his face. "My God," I cried inside, "Why?"

James had been drinking, again. It had been a domestic quarrel. He didn't deserve to die over a quarrel with his wife. Besides, he loved Joyce. Unfortunately, he'd gotten so drunk that he grabbed a butcher knife and threatened her. Frightened, she'd sent Rita, their eldest, for help. He'd just been laid off again. Joyce surely had known that it was his frustration that cursed her and jabbed at her and chased her around the table. She knew better than anyone else just who he really was, that behind the rage, behind the disappointment and the booze, was a large friendly man with a wide smile and warm brown eyes full of kindness and patience.

I vividly remember the day I came to stay with James and Joyce. I'd already spent two weeks in the classroom training with one hundred other college-aged kids before we were scattered across southern rural America to fight a War on Poverty. I was twenty, fresh out of junior college, and anxious to get some field experience since my major had been Social Welfare. In the three weeks that followed, we'd live with "poor families" whom the government paid to house and feed us. Then we were turned loose and allowed to set up our own households in a poor community, where we had limited supervision.

I was a transplant, but James and Joyce immediately welcomed me as a friend and treated me as family. The night I arrived they'd prepared an extensive dinner. James loved to cook, and fried chicken was one of his specialties. I managed to force down the slimy okra and tried black-eyed peas for the first time. I'd never seen a watermelon with a yellow center, but I relished the juicy slices. They tasted the same as the red ones back home. We laughed over silly nothings as we sat around their weed-infested backyard and tried to see who could spit the slippery seeds the farthest.

I helped Joyce clean up, and we exchanged smiles as we watched James with the kids on the back porch. They were having a contest to see who could spit the watermelon seeds the farthest.

"I got myself a good man," Joyce confided in me as she put the leftovers in the refrigerator. "Yesiree, a real good man." She hummed contentedly as she wiped the cracked tile countertop and closed the chipped cupboard doors above the sink.

Later that night, while I was eating popcorn and watching TV with my new family, I noticed an odor. It was mildew, a smell I never got used to. For some reason, the kids' room, where I slept, didn't smell quite as bad. They'd given me a bed by the window, for which I was thankful. The boys, Sean and Cody, shared a double mattress across the room, while Rita slept in a black metal frame bed next to mine. Baby Olivia slept with her parents across the hall. A bare light bulb flickered above us and made the cold checkerboard linoleum shine.

Long after the children were asleep, I'd creep into my bed. I lay there in the quiet and studied the California ocean poster I'd tacked up on the wall. I hadn't thought to ask permission, as it seemed I was only adding another piece of paper to the already tattered wallpaper that was peeling off the wall, exposing more layers of varied patterns.

I closed my eyes and tried to remember my wallpapered room back home. I missed my old bumpy pillow. I even missed the sound of the 18-wheelers on the freeway near my home. Instinctively, I listened for the sounds of Mom and Dad closing up the house, sounds I'd grown up with, like the cat being tossed out the back door, the sound of water running in the bathroom, and the sound of Dad's slippers clippity-clopping down the parquet hallway.

I'd never shared a room before, but I was grateful for the sound of the children's quiet breathing. I listened to the crickets and the neighboring hounds yelping in the still country night. I cried and tried not to get mascara stains on the pillowcases.

After the first night, I tried to avoid middle-of-the-night excursions to the bathroom, where the household cockroaches would scamper over my feet when I flicked on the light. Often on the way to the bathroom, I'd hear the buzzing sound of the TV, its station gone off the air. Once, I started to turn it off, but caught a glimpse of Joyce and James, embracing on the couch in the soft glow of the snowy screen.

James transported milk for a local dairy, and Joyce worked as a nurse's aide in a rest home. At first I reported to a Vista supervisor, but she was quite ill and she'd turned over a lot of responsibility to the Vistas who'd been there longer. Some of them were unscrupulous and irresponsible. I spent the first week trying to figure out exactly what I was supposed to be doing. Then I met Kim. She'd come a month earlier and was already renting a duplex in the black section of town, not too far from my family's house. Her roommate's twelve-month stint was nearly up; then I was to move in.

Kim talked a lot, but I liked listening to her Brooklyn accent. She was full of energy. Those first few weeks with James and Joyce, she and I began setting up tutoring programs with the local high schools. Kim was a take-charge person with natural organizational skills. She was extremely bright, or so I thought until she took up with James's brother, Rodney.

Kim met Rodney the weekend of James's yearly barbecue. They'd encouraged me to bring a friend, so I'd asked Kim. All the relatives were there. Rodney spotted Kim and immediately came on to her. She wasn't about to discourage his attentions.

Rodney looked extremely handsome in his white cotton pants and bright new oxfords. His light brown skin was smooth beneath his white unbuttoned short-sleeved shirt. He looked rather cosmopolitan. He had the kind of eyes a woman could get lost in, and when he looked at you, it seemed he was looking right through you. He scared me, but Kim saw adventure.

I never really expected it to last. Kim was a college graduate, and Rodney never finished high school. He was a sharp dresser, and his body dripped with gold accessories. No one seemed to know where he got his money because he didn't have a job. It was none of my business, I told myself, as I watched Kim slip through the back gate, Rodney's arm already around her shoulder.

Evidently the relatives were watching too. Joyce's sister, Margie, approached me on the back porch. "What are you girls doing here in Tulsa?"

"I work for the Community Action Program. I'm a Vista Volunteer." I knew they were familiar with Vistas living in the area.

"But what do you do?" she pressed me.

"I, I'm . . ." I'd never really discussed my work with James and Joyce, and I did think it odd, but they never asked. How could I tell her, I thought, without sounding condescending, that I was there to help poor people, like her? "I'm working with young mothers who have dropped out of school to have their babies." I thought that sounded pretty concrete and even noble.

"Well, are you a teacher then?"

"No, I'm a volunteer," I shifted uneasily in my seat.

"Why did you come here? Tulsa is a long way off from California. Why'd a little white gal like you wanna live out here? Don't you got no pregnant white gals to tend to back home?"

My throat became very dry. Lately, I'd been wondering about that myself.

"Don't you know, she's here to help us poor black folks," her husband, who'd been eavesdropping, suddenly volunteered.

I felt my face redden. My throat tickled, and I coughed nervously.

"Leave the gal alone," Joyce's mom entered the fray. "What she does is her own business. Besides she ain't done nothing wrong."

Thank you, Grandma! I smiled weakly, then excused myself to get a glass of punch.

I'd stood accused before their eyes, accused of being white and middle-class, accused of being educated and having opportunities. That's when I first wanted to quit and go home. I'd apologize first; but for what, for being myself?

I still believed in commitments. I moved in with Kim. Rodney had mysteriously disappeared. We had fellow Vistas over for dinner. We went to movies and plays in Oklahoma City. We tried to cover our irregular world with bright paint and inexpensive wallpaper. We received government checks monthly, drove government cars, and carried Carte Blanche gas cards. We were paid a minimal salary, but we always had more to spend than our black neighbors had.

Kim spearheaded our project with young, pregnant high schoolers who'd dropped out of school. It was Kim's idea to tutor them, so they could maintain their grade level and be able to slip back into the system once their babies were born.

Every morning, we'd pick the girls up and drive them to the city library, where we'd tutor them in math, English, and history. Kim would blast the radio and hum and sway with the beat. She didn't seem to notice the deafening quiet in the back seat where the girls sat, their ballooned tummies resting on their young slim thighs, their eyes, brown swirls of liquid chocolate, fearful and questioning. I never felt they trusted us.

I'd lean over the seat. "Want to listen to something else?"

They'd all shake their heads from side to side.

"How about a stick of gum?"

"No thank you," one would say softly while the others stared out the window.

Kim orchestrated a lavish multiple shower. A mother of one of the girls volunteered her home. I stayed home in bed that day with a migraine, thankful I had an excuse to miss it. I'd skipped a few of our sessions with the girls but tried to convince myself that Kim was more than capable, as I lingered in bed until I couldn't sleep any longer. Still, I felt guilty as hell.

I was pretty faithful about writing home even if I wasn't always completely truthful. My letters were so optimistic, they could have been Kim's. Our four teenaged moms still came faithfully. The shower had been a huge success. I wrote letters about the Head Start Center, where I'd spend two hours in the early afternoons, helping white teachers instruct mostly black children. I didn't mind that the kids hung on me at recess. I'd swing them around like airplanes, and they'd braid my hair. It felt kind of nice to be someone's hero. Then, we'd occasionally get a call to drive welfare moms to clinics and doctor appointments or to pick up their monthly commodities.

I'd reread my letters before I sent them off, and I'd almost feel good about myself.

What I didn't tell my folks was that my enthusiasm had begun to wane. What I didn't tell them was that I was getting frequent migraines that had been knocking me out for a couple of days at a time. Also, I'd developed a strange itchy rash. I didn't tell them that I had begun taking muscle relaxants, then sedatives, so I could sleep at night.

And I didn't write them about Mary Haney, a sweet, frail six-year-old with cystic fibrosis, who lived in a damp one-room apartment with her single welfare mom and two younger siblings. They didn't own a car and her mom couldn't afford to take off during the week, so she'd wait until Saturday then call us for rides. After several weeks I began to resent her calls. We weren't required to work weekends. I wanted someone else to rescue Mary Haney. I was drying up.

I began waking up at four in the morning and feeling as if I'd already had three cups of coffee. Mary probably wouldn't even live to be a teenager. Yet, while she fought every day of her life for breath, I struggled with my lack of sensitivity and compassion. I'd grown weary of sitting on hard clinic benches and watching the stream of sick, poverty-stricken humanity on my free Saturday. I'd grown tired of sitting on their bumpy couches, waiting to take them places and shivering in their living rooms because they'd quit using their grocery money to pay utility bills. Still, their faces haunted me.

I was getting out in four months and returning home. They'd never get out. The thought depressed me. I was tired of looking at the wretched circle of poverty. I didn't want to think about Mary dying any more, so I began taking the phone off the hook.

One Friday night a group of us Vistas decided to go to a dance at the black junior high where two of us worked. I lived close by, so I told them I'd walk over and meet them. Halfway there, I was intercepted by a police car. The squad car had slowly passed me, and I'd seen the officer on the passenger side look over his shoulder at me. At the corner, the car made a U-turn and pulled up beside me.

"What are you up to, young lady?" the one on the passenger side asked me as he hopped out of the vehicle.

I could hear the other officer radioing in, "We've got a white suspect, female, looks to be in her early twen . . ."

Suspect? The blood drained from my face.

"Just what are you up to young lady?" the first officer repeated.

"Sir?" was all I could get out.

"May I see some kind of identification, please?"

I fumbled through my purse and gave him my California driver's license. "I'm on my way to meet some friends at a dance," I stammered.

"Sure you are, gal." Some spittle from his bulbous mouth sprayed my bare arms as he spoke. "May I see that a minute?" He pointed to my purse.

I wasn't sure he had the right to rummage through my personal belongings, but I was alone and scared and wasn't about to protest.

"What'd you do with the cash, lady?" He practically threw the purse back at me.

"Officer, I'm afraid I don't understand," I muttered. "I'm a Vista Volunteer. I can verify that if . . ."

He ducked his head into the squad car and gave my license to the officer on the radio, then turned to me and said, "I'm afraid you'll need to come with us, Miss."

"What. . . !" I cried.

"We've got your pimp down at the station. According to him, you've done pretty well tonight. So if you'll kindly get into the car, we'll have a nice long talk down at the station."

I was mortified. This couldn't be happening to me.

Just then, my Vista friends drove by in their navy blue van. One of the guys jumped out.

"Officer, what's the problem? Joanie, what's going on?" he blurted in one incensed breath.

Then the officer at the radio opened his door, walked around the car, and handed me my license. "I'm afraid we've made a mistake, young lady. It was just that you matched this fella's description perfectly."

"It was just . . ." I was close to tears. "It was just that you nearly arrested me!"

He turned to his partner. "Let's go, Bill. She's clean, works for the Cap Agency."

"That's what I told you!"

Bill, the one with the round fat lips, gave me a hard look. "Lookey here, young lady, let me give you a piece of advice: decent white gals have no business in this neighborhood."

My friend grabbed me by the elbow. "Let's get out of here."

Instead of going to the dance, we went for pizza. After we'd talked for a few hours, and they'd gotten me reasonably calmed down, they drove me home. The place was completely dark. I was grumpy with Kim for forgetting to leave the porch light on. In the moonlight, I fumbled for my keys at the door. I tried to open it quietly in case she was asleep on her sofa bed in the living room. As the door creaked open, I was startled to see a naked black figure jolt from Kim's bed and run back through the house. I stood there momentarily paralyzed, not knowing if I should run in or run out. Within seconds, I heard the back screen door slam.

"Joanie, what are you doing?" She sat up clutching the bed sheets about her, clearly exasperated with my unexpected intrusion.

"Me?" I said, my body still trembling.

I never did tell Kim about the police incident. After that, she was never around much anyway. We still worked together and she tried to be civil, but she knew how I felt about Rodney, and she called me a snob.

At least Rodney had the horse sense to stay away when I was around. But sometimes I'd catch him leaving as I was driving up to the house. I noticed that his wardrobe had begun to deteriorate. That's when I knew his source of revenue had been cut off. I figured Kim was sneaking him in to feed him while I wasn't around, when she was supposed to be at work with me.

Kim became moody, tense, and sharp with me. She'd leave things strewn all over the house. She quit putting her makeup on and would wear the same thing for days.

I'd find cigarette butts in the unflushed toilet bowl, half-eaten bowls of cereal sitting on the kitchen table, and the closed, stuffy house would reek of body odor. I'd know Rodney had been there that afternoon.

The place was beginning to remind me of a bus station. I never knew when either of them would be there. Kim lost all interest in her job. Sometimes she'd be gone for days. And that was easy to do as no one ever checked up on us.

I began to hate Kim. I hated her lazy boyfriend. I hated the system that led me to believe that I could make a difference. I was tired of hanging around poor folks and hated Kim for changing, for giving up. I hated myself for not being able to hack it and wanted out.

One day, when Kim wandered into work late, with alcohol on her breath, I cornered her. "We've got to talk."

"OK." Her eyes watched me through narrow slits.

I grabbed her arm. "Are you on something, Kim? What'd Rodney give you?"

"Nothing!" She quickly jerked her arm away. "You want to talk? Right now?"

"No, tonight, and don't be late. I want to get some sleep tonight." The sedatives had begun to lose their effectiveness. I'd begun to wake up sporadically through the night.

I watched impatiently for her headlights to flash in the front window of our duplex. While I was brushing my teeth, I heard the car door slam.

She let herself in, and I sat down on the edge of her bed.

She sank down beside me. "OK, what is it? Shoot."

At least she was sober. I looked down at her long slender arm and, for the first time, saw the dark needle marks which dotted her pale skin. I had to tell her anyway.

"Kim, I'm leaving this Friday."

"But your time isn't up, not for a couple of months."

"I know, but I've made up my mind. We don't fit in, Kim, we never did. We don't belong here."

"Speak for yourself."

"Look at you, Kim." I was close to yelling at her. "Have you looked at yourself in the mirror lately? I mean, have you taken a good look? You're going downhill. You're losing it. We're both losing it. Leave with me before it's too late."

"Rodney and I are getting married. We're going to live here for a while. I'm in no hurry to return to Brooklyn."

I noticed that her eyes were pitifully small. They'd become dull and clouded. I blankly said, "Whatever makes you happy."

Kim drove me to the airport but didn't get out. She didn't say she was sorry. For anything. I felt bad about leaving her, but she was "free, white, and twenty-one," and there wasn't a damn thing I could do to save her.

My plane landed at San Francisco International on time, though we'd fought thunderstorms the whole way. Dad took my luggage, and Mom held my hand as we wandered about the top deck looking for our car. I lifted my face to the cool bay breeze and filled my lungs with its fresh salty air.

As far as they knew, I'd come home early because I'd been ill, and that was largely the truth. We talked of my adventures as our car sailed over the San Mateo bridge, through Castro Valley, and dropped into the lush hills of Pleasanton. I was selective about what I shared. I wanted them to be proud of me. I believed they'd have understood, anything. But how could I make them understand things I didn't understand myself, not yet anyway?

Dad told his silly jokes while I rested my face against the car's maroon velour interior. Perhaps I'd go back to school, get a part-time job. I'd try to forget. I nestled my body into the car's soft bulky folds.

I had tried to bury my experiences in middle America, but they'd surfaced anyway. Kim's phone call brought it all back. Waves of panic continued to assault me. I couldn't raise my head off the table. I heard a tapping noise at the kitchen window and turned my head to see a dark face peering in at me. It was James. I blinked. There was Joyce, then Kim, then Rodney. My head was spinning, then suddenly my world went black.

I must have been out for seconds. Lying on the cool floor with my head throbbing worse than before and my hip and knee feeling like they'd been kicked by a horse, I thought I heard Dad's voice.

"Merle, you must have startled her when you rapped on the window."

"Joanie!" Mom cried, and knelt down on the floor beside me. "What on earth . . ."

I tried to open my eyes, but they felt heavy. Mom set my head on her lap. Her hands were soft as she gently caressed my face.

"Dad, she looks like she's seen a ghost." Mom sounded scared.

Dad knelt beside us. "Joanie, open your eyes, talk to us, dear."

I wanted to open them. I wanted to let them know I was all right. Still, I didn't want to face the memories or deal with my emotions. But even with my lids closed, I could see the concern and worry on their faces. It was time to tell.

Interview

1. *Approximately what percentage of "Intruders" is factual?*
I'd say 50 percent.
2. *About what percentage of the events in your short story is your experience?*
I'd say 75 percent on that.
3. *How many short stories had you written before you wrote "Intruders"?*
Eight.
4. *How did you plan your story?*

When I decided to write my story, I first jotted down a long list of Vista experiences. I put them in four groups: the family I lived with, Kim, problems with the poor community, and inner conflicts. Then I wrote the first page and ending paragraph of the story. I chose Kim's news of James's death as a springboard because it was an attention-getter and it immediately put tension into the story. After that, I wrote a very rough, incomplete draft.

The fourteen screen cards I wrote next (see pp. 70–73) were fairly detailed because I had an abundance of ideas and was not yet sure what I would cut or keep. Sometimes I wrote new ideas on a side sheet of paper. Examining my scene cards, I saw racial tension, idealism, culture shock, and disillusionment. Wanting to blend those issues but realizing I needed to make major cuts, I pulled the cards that best showed these issues and wrote a complete rough draft from them.

5. *What were the major steps you went through in writing and rewriting your story?*

a. First draft: wrote out story longhand using scene cards as rough outline (see above).

b. Made revisions on handwritten copy.

c. Second draft: typed the handwritten copy.

d. Husband read and made notations.

e. Third draft: made revisions on typed copy (combination of husband's suggestions and my own revisions).

f. Fourth draft: reread, used Wite-Out, revised some more, typed corrections over Wite-Out, made copies for group.

g. Fifth draft: took story home after group discussion; made revisions on every page; considered Professor Phillips's comments, the graduate student assistant's feedback, and my group's comments; also made a lot of my own changes.

h. Turned in story for grading.

i. Sixth draft: took graded copy and revised a final time for submission to "Scripts and Stories" [class materials for the following fall creative writing course]; later revised the story again for possible publication.

6. *In rewriting your story, what helped you the most?*

Professor Phillips and the graduate student assistant for the course wrote specific reactions and suggestions on my early draft. My husband read the story carefully and also made specific notations. Members of my group came up with little detail changes I hadn't considered. When I realized some of their impressions of my story were different than I'd intended, I made some revisions and tried to make my story clearer. I never realized before the course with Professor Phillips how important rereading, constructive feedback, and rewriting were.

Scene Cards for "Intruders"

1.
Parents home—patio breakfast
Joanie surrounded by love, warmth, familiarity
Allusion to intrusive phone call

2.
Phone call—intrusion
Kim—unexpected, unwanted call
Joanie tells us about Kim—some background (marriage?)
Kim drops hint, "If it was a white boy, it wouldn't have happened"
Joanie calls out to parents—"Long distance"
Joanie lies to Kim—wants to forget past. Hasn't told parents everything

3.
Joanie sits at kitchen table—feels sweaty, weighed down—reconstructs what Kim has told her about killing for our benefit. (Happened in kitchen)
Joanie compares Tulsa kitchen to her home one (refrigerator?)

4.

Flashback begins

Background—recall how it started

Idealist—run-in with reality

Training—100 college kids—6 weeks not enough to prepare one for the reality of culture shock

Transport white middle-class city girl to black poverty-stricken rural America

Poverty only part of problem—lack of education, ignorance, prejudice, culture, youth

5.

Arrive at James and Joyce's house—6-week stay

Slight physical description

Kind of parents they were—husband/wife relationship

Govt. pays them—both work—four kids—share bedroom

Joanie hammers poster on wall

Cockroaches—end of first night

Mildew odor—smell of poverty

6.

Vista friends

Kim—characteristics—things we did (people to dinner, decorate place, normalcy to our irregular world, hand wallpaper, movies, circus, plays—they're cosmopolitan, GSA cars, Carte Blanche credit cards, freedom)

Even though we didn't make a lot of money—always had more than they did. (First chasm)

7.

Gulf widens at their house (when relatives come—their accusations—their eyes). Joanie the invader—intruder—she wants to apologize for being herself. "They hate me."

Grandmother takes Joanie fishing—tries to be kind—sit in dumpy area. They think it's great. Joanie doesn't fit in—starts to get headaches

Joanie wants to take bath—has to take diapers out of tub—kids think bath is a novelty. Brush teeth, "why you do that?"—never seen floss

Joanie has own bed—Vista friend shares bed with child who wets bed

8.

Joanie moves in with Kim

Sent out by area supervisor—liaison with high school—(dropouts and
    school)—teenage pregnant mothers happier than Joanie—they have
    families. She's terribly homesick.

Father of one daughter condescending

Mary Haney—poor white girl—hospital clinic—on call (resentful).
    Hospital/clinic daughter cystic fibrosis. Lives in narrow dark room
    kitchen, living and sleeping areas all together. Kids on welfare. "So glad
    I can call you" (mother). Feeling guilty for not wanting to be
    involved—take phone off hook

Mildew smell, unwashed clothes, dampness, unbathed kids

Water turned off—phone disconnected (the Haneys)

Birth of Olivia—regal name, princess—will never get out—sentenced to
    poverty

Police stop me on way to dance

Taxi man questions my character because of neighborhood I give as
    address

9.

Kim's boyfriend—imposing—never leaves—find out he's one of James's
    relatives

Kim & Randy ask me to go for weekend to Texas—so lonely, I go. Stopped
    by police. "Two white gals—one nigger" over radio. "You girls O.K.?"
    Stopped again at a Frosty Freeze—interrogated—questioned—arrested

Mortified, humiliated, fearful of being in tight area

Kim and I one cell/ Randy in other—Hate Randy—Joanie doesn't think
    she was prejudiced, but she is. Hates it about herself

Randy's lazy, talks slow, Kim's not too bright either—she's a fool—what a
    mess—I should never have come along—I want to go home—dare not
    call folks

Police check GSA—call Houston headquarters—humiliated—don't want
    to be around black folks—even poor folks. Overhear police call us
    poor white trash

10.
Things not the same when I get back to Tulsa

Kim hardly ever comes home at night, moves some things out—doesn't
communicate—Joanie isolated, practically alone—foreigner in
American city

Two months go by—made a commitment—hang in there. Heart not in it.
Depression sets in, disillusionment—anger

Kim takes pay, drops out, doesn't work. No one checks up on us

11.
Kim sees me off at airport. Leaves Randy home sleeping—his main
function in life. She looks down at my baggage and says "I'm sorry."
Joanie tries to understand. "It's all right"

Joanie has lost any real feeling. Lost ability to be honest with herself

12.
The plane pulls out of the storm

Dad carries luggage to car. She inhales fresh misty bay air. They want to
hear all about her adventure as car sails over San Mateo bridge and
across freeways—drop down into lush hills of Pleasanton. She's
selective about what she says. Can't tell them everything. I can't tell
them about the dull throbbing ache—I don't understand. I must
protect them. I must protect me. They expect to see sun-shining Joanie
walk off that plane. I can't let them down

13.
Climbing into Dad's polished car—proud of it

Deep in the recesses of my generous upbringing. I know they'd understand
anything and what they couldn't understand they'd try to understand

Dad told his silly jokes all the way home. The interior leather smell of the
car smells sweet. I'll get a job—Mom "sounds like it was a good
experience for you"

14.
Back in kitchen—today
Heart races—anxious feeling

6. Stories

Goals and Means

Goals

Every day, writers—beginners and pros—start a poorly conceived story that is doomed to fail. It need not be that way. Although writing and rewriting an effective story is time-consuming, it is worth the effort because a well-thought-out short story entertains, expresses some of life's limitless experiences, and involves readers intellectually and emotionally.

Whether storytellers are aware of it or not, the urge to tell stories is—as Robert Crichton has said—natural, vital, intuitive, and ageless. From time to time, everyone feels this need. For some of us, though, it is more than a passing urge. It may become a hobby, or it may become a way of life and a means of supporting one's self. Whatever the case, it does become a way to share a view of life's plenty. In its selection, invention, and arrangement of events, a story also imposes order on life and helps both writer and readers make sense of it.

The best short stories mirror life, showing people with goals and problems. "Crooked Handlebars" (chapter 3) shows two main characters who are lonely. In "Treason and Vengeance" (chapter 4) Gabriella wants romance and affection but faces problems attaining them. Stories that come to life show life and let readers extrapolate meanings; they are not written primarily to prove a point or to illustrate meanings (or to get even with someone, such as an ex-spouse or former lover).

The successful short story also involves the reader. To do so, the story must hold the reader's interest in the opening lines. If it is to be funny, it must be so early in the story. During the opening paragraph is not too soon.

Many effective stories have one or two intriguing characters, such as Joanie in "Intruders" (chapter 5). Some stories involve readers by including a character that we come to care for. Readers need not like the main characters, but they need to at least find them fascinating.

It's important not to insult your readers' intelligence but rather require them to read carefully. If points in the story are obvious, readers feel superior and distanced; they may feel offended. On the other hand, if the story is told subtly, readers must stay alert. By discovering significant details, they will take pleasure in their findings. They will stay involved. (More about obviousness and subtlety below.)

By considering your readers early, you will solve some of the problems that every writer faces between those first blank sheets of paper (or the lonely, nagging cursor on the computer screen) and the final draft. As you write and rewrite, you must ask yourself repeatedly: Who will be my readers? What can be left out? What needs to be shown in detail? You must understand your readers if you are to write a story that will entertain them, mirror life, and involve them intellectually and emotionally.

Once you have considered your readers, you should think about how much to include and how obvious to be or how subtle.

A beginning writer once wrote a story about a married woman who was dissatisfied with an old station wagon she and her husband owned and who was envious of another couple who owned a better house and car. By the end of the story, however, the main character felt closer to her husband, and her situation did not look so hopeless after all. In the last scene, the couple drive off in their old station wagon with the license plate FMLYWGN, which is an effective conclusion to the story. It's also subtle because, at story's end, readers have to figure out that the wife and husband are a family, not dissatisfied individuals. (Readers may also remember that this is the same car that the woman was unhappy with at the beginning of the story.)

Depending on the readers, this story's writer could have been more obvious or more subtle. An obvious ending that assumes inattentive or unintelligent readers: the woman comments to her husband, "Well, this old car doesn't look so bad after all." That's about as obvious as you can get. A more subtle ending: omit mention of the license plate altogether as the couple drives off in their old station wagon and expect readers to remember the wife's initial unhappiness with the car.

Whether they are aware of it or not, writers repeatedly choose how obvious or how subtle to be. Writers should make those decisions after they consider how perceptive their readers are likely to be.

If you write mainly for a small group of readers—and you will be as you write most of your first short stories—you should write for attentive and intelligent adults, readers who get the point the first time, or surely the second. Generally, readers of short stories do not want to read stories about life as it appears in television or popular movies.

Means

Settings

Beginning writers often give little thought to settings. If you read drafts of their work, they frequently do not indicate where the scenes take place. If the locations are indicated, they are rarely described vividly. In their descriptions of settings, beginning writers typically present either blurry pictures or no pictures at all.

As is illustrated in "Crooked Handlebars" by Pappy's dirty, neglected, and disorganized home, the living space or work quarters of the main character often reveal what the character is like. In addition, settings sometimes establish the mood of the scene and the writer's attitude toward the character (for example, satirical).

As in movies and plays, the lighting in a story can also affect mood and meaning. Note how the absence of bright light in the conclusion of "Treason and Vengeance" reinforces the mood of loss and loneliness: "He slams the door behind him. The light bulb in the living room burns out, and the house is dark and quiet. Gabriella lies on the floor with her eyes wide open. The moonlight illuminates her motionless silhouette."

Sometimes sounds can be a significant aspect of a setting, as in this passage from "Intruders":

I even missed the sound of the 18-wheelers on the freeway near my home. Instinctively, I listened for the sounds of Mom and Dad closing up the house, sounds I'd grown up with, like the cat being tossed out the back door, the sound of water running in the bathroom, and the sound of Dad's slippers clippity-clopping down the parquet hallway.

I'd never shared a room before, but I was grateful for the sound of the children's quiet breathing. I listened to the crickets and the neighboring hounds yelping in the still country night. I cried and tried not to get mascara stains on the pillowcases.

Clothes can also reveal a character's personality and moods. In "Intruders," for example, Rodney's flashy clothes are gradually replaced by shoddy ones as he drifts deeper into drugs and poverty.

Most descriptions of settings are not as detailed as the description of Pappy's home in "Crooked Handlebars." Some stories say little or nothing about lighting, sounds, or clothing, but when you want to show someone's character or help establish a mood while cueing readers about how to react, using those aspects may be an effective option.

Characters

In stories, we learn about characters mainly from their actions and words (and perhaps occasional thoughts or brief analysis from the author). Not that characters explain themselves to us; they act and interact. We readers see the characters; we figure them out.

How to introduce your characters? Shakespeare often began his plays in mid-conversation, either shortly before something was about to happen or shortly after an important occurrence. He knew how to catch and keep the viewer's (reader's) attention.

Fairly early in a short story, readers need to know two things: who the main character is and what he or she wants. In "Treason and Vengeance," for example, readers can quickly see that Gabriella wants romance and affection but is not getting them. Many beginning writers fail to reveal these two essentials, and readers flounder for page after page wondering if they missed something. Or they quit reading the story.

Skillful writers also create obstacles that hinder the character's progress. In "Crooked Handlebars," both Nick and Pappy want companionship, but Nick's caution and mistrust are the main barriers to their eventual tentative friendship. In "Treason and Vengeance," Gabriella wants romance and affection, but both men, especially Charles, are more inclined to offer Gabriella sex. In "Intruders," Joanie initially wants to succeed in her Vista work in Oklahoma; later, she wants to return home and find peace and comfort. In her Vista work, she faces many demoralizing setbacks then, once she is home, struggles to repress her troubling memories and emotions rather than confide in her parents, to whom she is close.

When the central character seems true to life (wants something, yet runs into problems in getting it), readers stay interested. Conflict and problems attract and hold readers. As Lajos Egri points out, "Since most of us play possum and hide our true selves from the world, we are interested in witnessing the things happening to those who are forced to reveal their true characters under the stress of conflict" (Egri 1960, 181).

Beginning writers sometimes create stories with several indistinct main characters, and their stories lack focus and force. However, most successful short stories have only one main character ("Intruders"), two central characters ("Crooked Handlebars") or, occasionally, three main characters ("Treason and Vengeance"). Because story time is so limited in a short story and because it takes time to develop or reveal a character, it's usually important to focus on no more than a few characters. For a story to hold reader interest, we must care about the main character or at least be interested in it. And, in most stories, the character must seem so lifelike that we forget that the story is fictional.

Often, first-time writers make the mistake of allowing the main character to achieve too much or change too drastically during a brief story time, but, as in "Crooked Handlebars," a short story should resolve little. For example, if the major character has problems at both work and home, it would be preposterous to show success in both areas; that's hard to accept in the limited time span that short stories cover.

When you study short stories, you will notice that many have a main character seeking a goal, coming up against obstacles to reaching the goal, then a resolution of either achieving it or not (Figure 2). Sometimes, as in "Crooked Handlebars," the conclusion hints that the main characters will eventually achieve their goals.

Means of Perception, Person, and Tense

The following passage is adapted from a short story draft:

Stacy was one of the kids in the group, the only girl in the group of boys, who towered over her. Most of the guys were three to five years older than her, but she didn't care. Mary had plans of her own—chasing fireflies and playing "statues" with Juanita and Angela. They were too busy throwing each other around on Juanita's front lawn to notice Stacy, who knew Mary wanted nothing to do with her anyway.

character seeks goal → conflicts/problems ——→ success/failure

Figure 2. Basic structure of most short stories

In this excerpt, the author has told readers about the thoughts and feelings of more than one character. We are told that Stacy didn't care that the boys were older than she; then what Mary plans to do; then that three girls were so busy playing that they did not notice something; finally we learn what is going on in Stacy's mind again.

In short stories, especially within the same section of a story, shifts in the means of perception or viewpoint are distracting, even confusing. They are rarely made in published contemporary short fiction. It diffuses attention; it prevents the reader from getting to know well one character and his or her thoughts, perceptions (what the character sees or hears, for example), and emotions. As Rebecca Rule and Susan Wheeler advise, "We urge you to limit yourself to telling one person's story, at least when you are new to writing fiction or until you've studied several stories told from more than one perspective" (Rule and Wheeler 1993, 186).

You might tell your story from the first person point of view, as in "Intruders": "Mom sat down next to me and gave my hand a big squeeze. Dad took my other hand in his and offered a word of prayer." The first person *me* and *my* refer to a fictional character in the story. Rarely is a story told from the second person point of view, a fictional *you*. Often it is narrated from the third person point of view, as in "Treason and Vengeance": "Gabriella comes to the sofa and sits next to Charles. She caresses his face and plays with his curly hair."

A story is often told in the past tense, as in "Crooked Handlebars," or occasionally in the present, as in "Treason and Vengeance." Critics and teachers give differing opinions about the consequences of choosing among means of perception, person (first, second, or third), and tense (present or past). Nearly all agree that in a short story, especially if you are new to writing them, you should be consistent throughout. For example, use one character as the means of perception and the third person past tense throughout the story. Or use a different character as the means of perception and first person present tense. Or some other choice, as long as it is followed consistently.

Dialogue

While stories need not have dialogue, they usually do because dialogue—what is said and how it is said—is a miracle of life and storytelling.

Consider a scene from a story titled, "The Killing Field," by a former student, Steve Swanson:

> As we left the restaurant and started the walk home, a sense of euphoria filled my entire being. "What did you think of Karen?" I asked Chris.
> "She's nice."
> "You think she's cute?"
> "Yeah. Sure."
> "I think she likes you."
> "Maybe."
> "You think Michelle likes me?"
> "Could be."
> "You don't think she does?"
> "I didn't say that."
> "You didn't say much of anything."
> "I think she likes you."
> "Cool."

First, dialogue should reveal what the main character is like, what he wants, and the progress or lack of progress toward achieving such goals. In the scene above, the narrator is the main character, and his dialogue clearly reveals that he finds Michelle attractive and wants his friend, Chris, to reassure him that Michelle likes him.

Second, what characters are like and what they want should most often be expressed indirectly in dialogue, because what people say is often oblique, complicated, subtle. We say one thing when we mean something else, and we seldom come right out and say what's important to us. In the scene from "The Killing Field," Chris does not want to talk about the two young women he and the narrator have recently dated, but he does not say so directly: he doesn't say "I don't want to talk about it." He gives short, unengaging answers to avoid a detailed discussion. Effective dialogue tells us only enough to get us interested; then we figure out the situations for ourselves. That way we become—and stay—involved with the characters.

Finally, as the scene above illustrates, dialogue should usually be concise. Although everyday conversation contains unnecessary words and insignificant pauses, stories should not. The dialogue in the scene from "The Killing Field" seems natural and yet less wordy and more revealing than actual conversation. Note, also, that effective dialogue contains only one point in each speech because readers can grasp only so much at a time. What Raymond Hull says about dialogue in plays applies to dialogue in fiction as well: "A general rule is that each speech must convey only one idea. This is not a stylistic quibble; it is a practical necessity. Readers cannot grasp complicated speeches. You must feed them information as a bird feeds its young, piece by piece, and you must allow time for the digestion of each piece" (Hull 1983, 106).

Structure

Figure 2 illustrates the basic structure of many short stories. By failing to emulate that structure, many beginning writers write excellent scenes yet come up short when their stories have been completed. Structural flaws ground their flight.

1. *One or two—or occasionally three—main characters seek a goal.* The story may have more than three major characters; in a short story, this usually confuses the reader and lessens the story's impact. The central character (or characters) may not have a goal or may seem to have several unrelated goals. Main characters don't usually say what the goal is directly, but readers should be able to figure it out quickly.

2. *The character (or characters) experiences problems or conflicts while trying to reach the goal.* The central character may not face enough difficulty when trying to reach the goal: perhaps there are not enough conflicts or complications. Who would want to read a story that shows the main character getting cooperation from nearly everyone? Alternately, the story may have too many problems crammed into a short period (like a soap opera).

3. *The character usually succeeds or fails to reach the goal.* The story may veer off course and skid to a halt in front of an unrelated matter. Or, it may show us an ending that is inconsistent with the character or situations that have been described earlier in the story.

Often, we see only briefly how the main character reacts to reaching or not reaching the goal, as in the ending of "Treason and Vengeance," where Gabriella is reduced to lying motionless on the floor, illuminated only by moonlight. Occasionally, we also learn how others react to the main character's success or failure.

With so many ways for a story to go wrong structurally, is it any wonder so many stories fail?

Many writers begin telling their stories too soon, leaving readers to wait for the real story to begin. To avoid this pitfall, after you write a first or second draft, see if the story works better by deleting the first paragraph (or two or three or four). As Chekhov wrote, "My own experience is that once a story has been written, one has to cross out the beginning and the end. It is there that we authors do most of our lying" (Engle 1982, 55).

Above all, a story's beginning needs to engage readers, to hook them, so that they begin to be caught up in the story and want to read more. A beginning also needs to avoid unimportant details. Consider the opening of "Intruders":

> Mom sat down next to me and gave my hand a big squeeze. Dad took my other hand in his and offered a word of prayer. I closed my eyes and felt the warm sun on my face. The delicious scent of sweet william filled the morning air. Life had returned to normal.

From this opening paragraph, readers learn information that will prove to be important as the story develops: the narrator is close to her parents, it is a religious family, the narrator is now appreciative of the warmth and fragrance of nature, and, most importantly and most intriguingly, "life had returned to normal." Right away, readers are hooked and want to know what has gone wrong earlier.

Nearly all effective short stories refrain from trying to cover a long story time because doing so can weaken dramatic effect. For example, when selected events from different years are shown in a twenty-page story, the story lacks unity and punch. The story time of "Crooked Handlebars" is less than a full day. The story time of "Treason and Vengeance" seems to be only a few days. There, as in many stories, the reader cannot figure out the story time precisely.

Many stories change mood from time to time. No matter which mood is dominant—tension, melancholy, humor, whatever—lack of variety can be tedious. In most serious stories, at least one scene has humor. In most effective humorous stories, some scenes have moments of seriousness. "Crooked Handlebars," for example, contains a range of emotions: some scenes are amusing; some subdued and melancholic.

Successful stories also omit some action. In "Intruders," readers are not shown Joanie's Vista training, merely told that it lasted only two weeks. Stories should exclude what is unimportant to the characters, to the story's structure, and to meanings. It's also important to end a scene before it wears out its welcome. As Alfred Hitchcock reportedly said sometime ago, "The one who tells you everything right away is a bore."

Contrary to what many beginning writers seem to believe, most effective stories—especially short ones or ones covering only a few days of story time—avoid flashbacks. Writers should hesitate before using flashbacks. In the first place, flashbacks can confuse readers. In the second place, flashbacks seem a little old-fashioned; current stories rarely use them, and you may give the impression of being behind the times if you do. Using a flashback in a story can be like using a soliloquy in a modern play. In the third place, some writers resort to flashbacks because they think readers need to know something of the character's past when they don't.

Imagine that "Crooked Handlebars" included scenes of Nick being beaten by his father. That could disrupt the story, lessen its focus, and detract from its subtlety. Occasionally, as in "Intruders," a flashback may be effective. In that story, the flashback structure assures that the story begins at a moment of high drama and mystery: the report of a death that is upsetting to the story's main character and intriguing to the reader.

Finally, an effective ending is crucial. The ending should make sense, given the characters and their previous actions. An effective ending will not guarantee the success of your story, but an ineffective one will sabotage it.

Meanings

A basic urge all writers bring to fiction . . . is the desire to make sense of the random, chaotic, painful, terrifying, astonishing events of our lives. . . . We want there to be some sense of events, even if the sense is that no one is in charge and entropy conquers; that all is illusion or a baroque and tasteless joke. (Piercy 1999)

Every story has meanings. Its characters—their actions and interactions—reveal general characteristics of human behavior. The best stories show some of the complexity and subtlety of human nature, such as the tentativeness of forming new friendships ("Crooked Handlebars") or the conflicting emotions within a character ("Intruders"). A story usually has several meanings. And sometimes readers see meanings that the writer wasn't aware of or didn't intend. That is one of the wonders of telling stories and learning what people see in them.

In a well-written story, characters do not tell readers what the story means (a sign that the writer is uncertain of the story's effectiveness). Instead, readers discover the story's meanings. That way, the readers become more involved in the story and more impressed—by the story, by the writer, and, not insignificantly, by themselves.

Limitations and Possibilities of Short Stories

For a short story, the key word is *limited.* Settings, characters, structure, and meanings: all of them must be limited.

Typically, a short story should not have many detailed settings; otherwise, the reader sees none well and learns little from them.

The number of characters must be limited, too. Otherwise, the reader gets to know none of them well and remains a passive, at best vaguely interested, bystander.

The structure of a short story should also be restricted. An effective short story's scenes are usually arranged chronologically and show significant events in the life of the main character (or characters) during a few days or less.

Because meanings are largely determined by setting, character, and structure, if those three components are limited, the meanings will be, too. If not, it can be a bewildering task to understand the points or meanings of a short story.

In some ways, short stories are more restricted than novels (for example, fewer major characters and fewer story lines); however, short stories are not the novel's impoverished cousins. The limitations of short stories, especially their brevity, make for potential strength. Because they are brief and can be read repeatedly, short stories can be more compressed, elliptical, symbolic, and ambiguous. They can be more demanding of their readers than novels, but very rewarding, too.

Short stories can be like sonnets, which are severely constrained by form—in English, fourteen lines and approximately ten syllables per line, a fairly regular rhythm, and one of several tricky rhyme schemes. That's a confining space to work in, to say something important without sounding stiff or silly. Yet within that space can be found some of the most concise and memorable expressions of human belief and experience. Through the limitations of form, the sonnet forces the writer to work harder and better than ever. So does the short story.

Part Three

Writing Stories

When you say in fiction: "He bowed his head in shame," it is likely to be a lie. Or "he gripped the chair until his knuckles were white." When you write such a thing about a character, ask yourself: "Did he really do that? Have I ever seen *anyone* do that?" . . . When you have written a story and it has come back [from possible publishers] a few times and you sit there trying to write it over again and make it more impressive, do not try to think of better *words,* more gripping words. Try to see the people better.

—Brenda Ueland, *If You Want to Write*

Only that which does not teach, which does not cry out, which does not persuade, which does not condescend, which does not explain, is irresistible.

—William Butler Yeats,
 "J. M. Synge and the Ireland of His Time"

Before You Begin

In her audiocassette program *Yes! You Can Write* (Neeld 1986), Elizabeth Neeld describes an art contest involving thirty-one student artists who were given different drawing materials and twenty-seven objects. Each artist was given the same amount of time to paint a still life with any combination of the objects. During the allotted time, each artist was observed by someone else who wrote down what each artist did. After all the student artists had finished, independent judges evaluated their works.

The findings: the winners were those students who had picked up the most objects and explored them the longest. The winners, more often than the other contestants, also changed their minds about which objects to include. They more often changed the arrangement of the objects. They more often moved the objects to a different part of the room so that their paintings would have a different background. And they switched their media (watercolor to oil paint, for example) more often than others. In short, the winners spent much more of their allotted time making changes and considering the results.

I have seen the same results with writers. Those who remain open to possibilities, seek options, and test many of those options usually write more powerfully than those who quickly zero in on a story and stick with it, avoiding major surgery and making only cosmetic changes, no matter how long they work on the story.

As you plan, write, and rewrite, do not settle on your story too so~ will usually come into focus only as you experiment extensiv~ plan, write, and rewrite again and again. Only tl clearly what you have to show.

Beginning story writers sometimes tell me that t *themselves* and that they write for themselves. Writing pressing yourself, and it can be therapeutic. But writings done for yourself should not be shown to others. What you share with others should be written for *others*.

Because writing is so complex and personal, no writing technique will work for everyone all the time. Some of the suggestions in this part of the book will work for you. Some won't. Remember: in writing, as in friendship and love, whatever works is good.

7. Planning

Character Biographies

Before you write a first draft, even before you organize your material, be sure that you know your main characters well. One way to better understand the characters you plan to write about is to create character biographies. You could write about what might have been important experiences in your characters' lives, from childhood up through the time in which the story takes place. One short but effective variation on the character biography is the description of several key experiences that the characters have had.

Even if little of this biography finds its way into the final version of the story, inventing it does help some writers understand their characters more completely. It helps them spot vagueness, inconsistencies, and improbabilities. This is another technique you need to try a few times before you will know if it works for you. Before creating a discovery draft, synopsis, or set of scene cards (all three are described below), you might write a character biography. Or perhaps you will prefer to write the biographies after the first draft or at another step. You should be careful, however, to not spend too much time and energy writing character biographies. You don't want to tire of the characters before you write their story.

Playing "What if. . . ?"

Once you have written a vivid journal entry or performed a writing exercise about a topic that you know well and think you would enjoy developing, you could play "What if. . . ?" This means rereading the scene or scenes you have written, then quickly jotting down brief descriptions of scenes that could occur either before or after the scenes you have created, or both. As with freewriting, do not worry about errors. Do not stop to rewrite any-thing. Let your mind go. Quickly jot down brief descriptions of what might have happened before or after the scenes you originally wrote. After you have let your mind give birth to many possibilities, reread what you have written and select any situations that you want to write up as scenes. You may be well on your way to a first draft.

To illustrate the playing of "What if. . . ?" reread Sandi Mendonca's journal entry, "I'm Getting Married," on pp. 26–27. Next, consider these possibilities. Perhaps the reader should see an earlier scene where the man and the woman narrator decide not to date anymore. Maybe the reader should see them after he has been married for a few weeks and is already be-ginning to suspect he married the wrong woman. Maybe the reader should see the narrator decide to marry on the rebound (hastily marry someone she doesn't love). What if the reader saw a scene between the two women? Per-haps they dislike each other but try to hide it. Perhaps they like each other. What if a scene shows the other woman subtly turning the man against the narrator (in other words, the other woman is catty but he doesn't notice)? Might it be useful to show the reader part of a scene in which the man and the narrator are parked in a steamed-up car, letting their hands and lips do some communicating? Or it could be that the man and the woman narra-tor have a close, platonic friendship whereas the man has a powerfully sex-ual relationship with the woman he is going to marry. Maybe the narrator withheld sex whereas the fiancée gladly did not, or vice versa. Maybe the reader needs to see a scene in which the man and narrator have done some-thing they would regret. It could be they have hurt each other's feelings, whether deliberately or inadvertently. Maybe one of them tried to make the other jealous, and the scheme backfired.

Of course, there are many, many other possibilities. The point is to gen-erate a lot of them without judgment and to write them down quickly. After you have made a long list of possibilities, and maybe the next day after you have given your subconscious a shot at the job, you can decide which scenes you want to keep and how to arrange them. Eventually you will probably decide that many of the possibilities on your list are fruitless to pursue. That's OK. That's natural. What *is* important is to generate some promising possibilities, then explore them later.

Playing "What if. . . ?" in a group can also work well. I have used it with many groups, always productively. The trick is to generate possible scenes without pausing to consider their usefulness. Whether you work alone or in a group, create possibilities spontaneously and without interruption, then pause to consider the usefulness of what you have created.

Getting Organized

Nearly all experienced writers organize their material in some way before they write a first draft. They do so because in the long run it saves time and often leads to better results. Try arranging the parts of your story before attempting the first draft, but remember that the paths of writing have many byways, dead ends, and U-turns. Sometimes you cannot find the ending until you finish a draft or two. Remember also that you can spend too much creative energy on planning your story, then run out of steam before completing the first draft.

For some writers, it's a mistake to talk about a story before they write it. Their enthusiasm and momentum slip away before the story is on paper. I say "some writers" because, again, people do work differently. John McLaren writes, "Once I have the kernel of an idea, I spend a week or two playing with it, exploring plot mechanics. Then I ambush someone and ask for their comments. I catch them somewhere and say: 'Do you mind if I tell you a story.' I don't actually listen, though. I'm looking at their eyes as I speak because the eyes don't lie. If they glaze over at any point I know I have to do some reworking. It's only when I've tested the story in this way on five or ten people that I feel happy with the plot" (McLaren 1999). This procedure works for McLaren, and it may work for you, but you should guard against telling others your plans in detail before you write your story, or you may never write it. Some writers subconsciously avoid the hard work of writing by talking so much about what they plan to write that they lack the time or energy to write!

Organize then, but not to the point of exhaustion, before you launch into your first draft. There are three ways to organize your story: discovery drafts, synopses, and scene cards.

Discovery Drafts

One way to start finding the story you want to tell is to write one or more discovery drafts. To do so, write your story as quickly as you can. As with focused freewriting (see chapter 2), write rapidly without judging or rewriting what you write. As you write, do not worry about format, punctuation, spelling, or word choice. Do not worry about anything except the brief story of the main character or two or, occasionally ,three. As quickly as you can, describe where each scene takes place and who does what, who says what. If you write this draft on a computer, try turning off the monitor, or turning it down, so that you are not distracted by what you see on the screen. While you write a discovery draft, do not stop and allow your mind to gag the writing's creator and shove your mind's critic onto center stage.

When you finish this rough draft, instead of reading it, put it aside for a day or two. When you look at it in the fresh light of another day, you may see a promising beginning; the story may kick and cry for attention. If not, you may want to try a second discovery draft. If one of your discovery drafts twitches with life, you should reread it carefully then revise it.

Try reading your draft aloud. Are there too many characters? What is the main character's goal? Do we learn of it early in the story? What blocks his or her progress toward that goal? What helps progress toward it? Can any scenes be dropped? Do any scenes need to be added? Can any be shortened? Can scenes be placed elsewhere in the story with better results? What does the story show about motives and behavior?

If you dislike any of the answers to these questions, revise your draft. After that, if you are fairly satisfied with the results, skip the next chapter for now and read the chapter on rewriting (chapter 9). If, however, your discovery drafts are stillborn, try one or both of the remaining techniques below.

Synopses

Some writers create a synopsis or summary (or part of one) before doing the first draft. After you have written and revised your synopsis, read it aloud and have someone else read it to you while you visualize it.

Now ask these questions about your synopsis: Does the main character get lost in a crowd of characters? What is the main character's goal? Can readers figure it out early in the story? What blocks the main character's progress toward that goal? What helps the progress? Can any actions be omitted or shortened? Can actions be placed elsewhere in the story for a better effect? What is the story showing? Rewrite as necessary.

After you start to tire out or lose perspective, put the synopsis aside and do something completely different; return to it when you are alert and energetic. Rewrite, take a break, rewrite, take a break. . . .

When you are satisfied with the synopsis, you may make scene cards (as described below), or you may decide to divide your synopsis into scenes and write a first draft. If you write a synopsis, remember that you will probably make changes as you reach the final version of the story.

Scene Cards

Another way to organize a story is to write a description of each scene on a card (a 3-by-5-inch index card, for example), then revise some cards, add cards, delete others, and rearrange the remaining ones. If you have written a useful discovery draft or synopsis, you will probably want to base your scene cards on that. Let each card represent one scene or uninterrupted action in one continuous location. On each card, describe the setting, characters, and action concisely. Give snatches of dialogue if they come to you and you don't want to chance losing them (see Figure 3).

As you work with the scene cards, you need not write the scene descriptions in the order in which they will appear in the finished story. And if you have trouble getting a scene to come out right, don't allow yourself to become bogged down in it. Move on to other scenes, then return to the troublesome scenes. By then, chances are you will know better how to summarize them.

After you have described as many scenes as you can, ask the same questions that you asked about the discovery draft and synopsis. Make needed changes. Next, number the cards with a pencil and try pinning them up somewhere or laying them out on a table. Look again at your set of cards and ask the same questions that you applied before.

Try shifting a few cards around and rereading the results. If you are unhappy with the new story, you can go back to your original arrangement. If the new arrangement seems better, renumber the cards or assign a letter to each one and arrange them alphabetically. You should probably read and arrange the cards on different days. When you are fairly certain about the number, content, and arrangement of the scenes, you are ready to write a first draft. But as you do so, remember that your story is summarized on cards, not marble, and you will probably want to make further changes.

Most fiction writers like using scene cards (so do dramatists and scriptwriters), because the cards help writers structure their stories before they begin writing them.

When beginning writers read stories such as those in chapters 3–5, they may feel intimidated because they think they cannot include so many complexities and subtleties in their stories. Well, they shouldn't try to include

```
2. Kitchen

    Phone call—intrusion

    Kim—unexpected, unwanted call

    Joanie tells us about Kim—some background
        (marriage?)

    Kim drops hint, "If it was a white boy, it wouldn't have
        happened"

    Joanie calls out to parents—"Long distance"

    Joanie lies to Kim—wants to forget past. Hasn't told
        parents everything.
```

Figure 3. Sample scene card that describes a scene from "Intruders" by Claire Doud.

everything while planning their stories or, for that matter, as they write those first drafts. For most writers, in the early stages it's best to focus on the elements discussed early in the previous chapter: settings, dialogue, and actions.

Although symbols (if any) and other meanings, subtleties, and other refinements may emerge naturally as you write a first draft, don't count on it. You may feel the need to incorporate them later as you rewrite and rewrite the story. Don't try to do too much too soon. That way lies frustration, despair, perhaps even writer's block. For now, describe only settings, dialogue, and actions.

If you plan to base your story on a particular person and suspect that this person will recognize himself or herself in your fiction and be extremely upset by it, or if you plan to incorporate some material that others have written, you should read the next section. Otherwise, you are probably ready to turn to the following chapter and read about writing that first draft. Or, if you have written a promising discovery draft, you may want to skip the next chapter for now and move on to the chapter on rewriting (chapter 9).

Libel and Copyright

Because your story may be made public, you might need to consider some legal aspects. I don't mean to alarm you. Only rarely does a story present legal problems, but because a story could, you should understand the following issues before you write a story for publication.

Because I have not studied law, I can offer only general guidelines. If you think you might need legal counsel about a controversial or sensitive subject that you plan to go public with, then hire an attorney with expertise in libel. Similarly, if you are uncertain about copyrighted material that you would like to use in your story, see an attorney who specializes in copyright law.

If you base a character closely on a living person—as I have urged you to do—you should consider whether that person and others will recognize the source and take serious offense at your representation. If so, you could face legal pressures, or even a libel suit, especially if the person believes that he or she is recognizable and has suffered a damaged reputation because the character you created (and made public) committed illegal acts or behaved in antisocial or generally offensive ways.

In one instance, a woman claimed that the prostitute character in a man's novel was based on her. She sued him. A court ruled that the similarities between the person and the character were "insufficient to establish that the publication was of and concerning the plaintiff." The writer won; sometimes writers lose. Win or lose, such cases are time-consuming, expensive, and nerve-racking. And they have become more commonplace in recent years.

Writers should draw on people to infuse vitality into their characters. Perhaps the trick is to draw from real people but not too often and not too closely from anyone who might bring a lawsuit. Or maybe you want to use the small penis (or flat breasts) rule: "One way authors can protect themselves from libel suits is to say that a character has a small penis. . . . Now no male is going to come forward and say, 'That character with a very small penis, That's me!' " (Smith 1998).

Copyright matters are also complicated. Some issues have not been tested in the courts, and much of the application of the revised 1976 U.S. Copyright law to particular instances is uncertain. As a writer, you do not want to get bogged down in a legal swamp. But be aware that if your work is published, you must be careful about any previously written material you use.

In U.S. publications, you are free to quote from, or to paraphrase, material that was published before 1978 but never copyrighted or whose copyright has expired, although you are expected to acknowledge your sources. Most of the writings that were copyrighted before 1920 are no longer protected by copyright laws in the United States.

As a writer, normally you may also use selections from copyrighted works—including poems, song lyrics, and stories—but if you go public with your story, you will need permission from the current copyright holder, who may ask you to pay a fee.

By custom if not law, writers rarely seek permission for material they incorporate into writing they may do for either courses or writing groups. Often writers do not seek permission for material they incorporate into works that are published locally for no profit, though they should always acknowledge their sources (otherwise they are guilty of plagiarism). If you seek a large readership or income from your stories, or both, you should get permission from any copyright holder. If you don't, you chance a lawsuit for copyright infringement—or at least the threat of a suit. As a writer you have better things to do. Such as write.

Remember the benefits of relaxing after intense concentration and work. After planning your story but before launching into a first or later draft, you should probably take a long, diverting break.

8. Writing

> I know a good many fiction writers who paint, not because they're any good at painting, but because it helps their writing. It forces them to look at things. Fiction writing is very seldom a matter of saying things; it is a matter of showing things.
>
> —Flannery O'Connor,
> "Writing Short Stories," in *Mystery and Manners*

Circumstances

Once you have written a discovery draft, synopsis, or scene cards, or all three—or have begun to organize your material by an alternate method that works for you—you are ready to write the first draft. There is no single way to go about it. Writers work under different self-imposed conditions. One writer writes, "I have a study which is hopelessly messy and a laptop computer. My parrot Abraham sits with me, but the only contribution he ever makes is 'Uh-Oh'. I try to keep the room dark, with one little lamp on the desk. My cat is always underneath the lamp. There's a window behind me with a view on to our concrete backyard but I try not to look out—it's too dangerous" (Holman 1999).

Other writers work under yet other conditions of their own choosing:

Among the writers I have met, one habitually worked lying down in the dark, in a trailer with its windows painted black, dictating into a tape recorder. Another, when he wanted to think about a new novel, got on a bus to a destination about four hours away—it didn't matter where. When he arrived, he boarded another bus and rode back; by the time he got home, he would have the novel all plotted out. Another thought about a novel for three months, then sat down in a specially designed cubicle, smaller than a telephone booth, and typed furiously for thirty hours straight. When he came out, the novel was done. (Knight 1985, 10)

In matters of writing, perhaps especially in writing the first draft, whatever circumstances work for you are good.

One circumstance, however, is necessary for all writers: time set aside to work without distractions and interruptions. (I don't believe I have ever met or heard of a writer who liked to write a first draft with distractions and interruptions.) Without that clear stretch of road ahead, few writers get under way. Once under way, however, how they move forward is up to them.

Procedures

You have written journal entries, performed writing exercises, and found a promising source for a story. You have studied stories. By this time, you have begun to organize the story you plan to write and are in your favorite writing space at a propitious time. It's time to write the first draft of your story, but "your hands are shaky and your knees are weak," and it's not from being in love. What has gone wrong? Nothing. It's normal—in fact, beneficial—to be nervous before a performance, because nervousness can stimulate creativity. Accept it without becoming preoccupied with it, and begin writing. Don't wait for this feeling to go away. Don't talk about your nervousness. Begin writing, and you will get caught up in the writing and forget the nervousness.

The first draft of your story may consist largely of episodes from your life and the lives of others you know extremely well. You might stitch together a fictionalized version of an episode from your life; an episode much later in your life but one that you have added extensive details to; a fictionalized version of an episode from a parent's experience, one you have heard about over and over; and so forth.

The scenes in your first draft need to work together, to show one line of development, often one major character trying to achieve something. If the scenes are not connected, readers will be confused and remain uninvolved.

You may want to write a lot of journal entries about memorable experiences, then combine them into the first draft of a story. If you have already written journal entries for some of the episodes that make their way into your first draft, you can more likely breathe life into your story. Your previous writing about the episodes will have dredged up forgotten details: facts, sensations, feelings, and more. Now that you know the episodes better, you can make readers experience them, too.

When writing a first draft without a computer, try beginning each scene on a new page. If you later decide to rearrange scenes, or drop a scene, it will be easy and the results will not be messy. Double-space everything so you'll have room for revisions.

As we saw on p. 79 of chapter 6, you need to decide how to write your story: in the first person (an imaginary *I*) or in the third person *(he* and *she* and *they)*. If you are writing only your first or second short story, I urge you to write it in the third person. I do so because I have seen so many beginners write in the first person, then forget that the *I* is a fictional creation. Using *he* and *she* and fictional (not real) names will help most beginners stay focused on writing fiction, not inadvertent autobiography.

During the first draft, don't worry about grammar, spelling, punctuation, or the usefulness of what you are writing. For most people, being self-critical while writing is counterproductive. Writers use various ways to shut down the critic during the writing process.

Kent Haruf, author of the novel 'Plainsong' . . . wrote the first draft of the book with a wool stocking cap pulled down over his eyes. He would sit typing blindly in the unheated basement . . . trying to visualize the high, dry Colorado plains of his childhood. . . . His rather eccentric method was, he said, an effort to reach the emotional heart of his story unconstrained by the feeling that someone—an invisible critic—was watching over his shoulder and scrutinizing every word he chose. 'I was trying not to be analytical, to get in touch with the intuitive, the visual, the spontaneous, without any attention to detail and syntax,' said Haruf. . . . 'It takes away the terror when you're blind and you can't go back and rewrite a sentence,' he said. 'It calls for storytelling, not polishing.' (Smith 1999)

Television and movies often depict writers typing, ripping a sheet from the typewriter, then repeating this process over and over in frustration. Don't imitate television or the movies. While this is a dramatic scene, it is about the worst way to write, because the writers on television and movie screens are trying to write and rewrite at the same time. For nearly everyone, that's disastrous. Write; later, rewrite.

As you create the first draft and new material comes to mind, write it down. Later, when you reread and rewrite the story, if the new material does not fit in after all, you can delete it and store it in your journal or notebook. It's better to write when new material occurs to you and to cut during the rewriting stage than to disregard new material and struggle later to remember it.

If you don't know how to write a scene, skip it for now. If the trouble persists, your mind may be trying to tell you that there's a major problem with the story. If you feel like writing scenes out of order, that's OK, too, although if you don't use a computer, you should write scenes on separate sheets of paper that can be inserted into your story later.

If the creative fires smolder or die, don't despair. Do something else. Studies prove that sudden insights and surges of creativity often occur after intense efforts to create followed by a period of relaxation. You can achieve only so much during a writing session. Don't try to force the process, or you may get writer's block.

For some fiction writers, doing something else means doing a different type of writing, such as poetry. "Sometimes I say that if a writer works in more than one genre, the chances of getting writer's block are greatly diminished. If I am stuck in a difficult passage of a novel, I may jump ahead to smoother ground, or I may pause and work on poems exclusively for a time. If I lack ideas for one genre, usually I have them simmering for the other"(Piercy 1999).

Damon Knight explains how writers need to put their unconscious to work, then check back in with it from time to time, but not too often and not too urgently:

> If the unconscious isn't ready, don't push. If you do, you are like a chess player who keeps telling his partner what moves to make. If that goes on long enough, of course your partner is going to say, 'Well, play by yourself, then.' And there you are, making all the moves by yourself. (Serves you right.)
>
> To be productive, the unconscious needs a lot of stimulating input—odd facts or fancies to knock together, insights, specimens, interesting data of all kinds. . . .
>
> Critics talk about 'the well of inspiration,' and they say that the well sometimes runs dry. What this means, in my opinion, is either

that the author is feeling the lack of stimulating input, or that she has not given her unconscious time enough to think about the problem. Trying to force it is a mistake. (Knight 1985, 28–29)

Some people believe that nonverbal activity is especially effective for stimulating the writing process. A former student of mine said that riding her bicycle nearly always helped her figure out what she needed to write or rewrite. Dorothea Brande advises writers who want to recharge their creative batteries to "amuse yourself in wordless ways. Instead of going to a theater, hear a symphony orchestra, or go by yourself to a museum; go alone for long walks, or ride by yourself on a bus-top. . . . Books, the theater, and talking pictures should be very rarely indulged in when you have any piece of writing to finish" (Brande 1981, 133–34). If you read, Brande cautions, read material unlike what you are trying to write.

There is only so much you can achieve during the writing of a draft. E. L. Doctorow has compared writing with driving at night with the headlights on: there is not enough light to see very far ahead. Remember, too, that much of your first draft will probably need a lot more work. It usually does. As often happens when we take on a large and complicated task, we make errors and unwise decisions. It's OK. No mistakes, no progress. Don't allow yourself to get bogged down in the parts that don't seem to be coming out well.

If you cannot finish the first draft in one sitting, try stopping at a moment of high tension, maybe in the middle of a sentence. That may sound strange, but many writers find it easier to resume writing if they have stopped at a high point or in mid-sentence. At least they have something to begin with for the next session. Stacy Rahl told me that she often stops in the middle of a scene and writes a few notes to herself that she places in brackets. When she resumes writing, she has a scene to complete and some reminders.

People restart their writing in different ways. Peter Elbow advises writers to read some of their best previous writing aloud. "This gives you the actual psycho-muscular feeling for what it was like to put juice into words. By reawakening this memory/feeling, you can more easily get into that gear again. Reading over your own good work is particularly useful when you are having a hard time getting warmed up—perhaps after a long period of nonwriting" (Elbow 1981, 371). Other writers start a writing session by copying the last few pages of what they wrote during their last session. For them, this process builds steam: it allows them to review where they have been and to move on to new territory. Still others write quickly, for ten minutes or so, about whatever comes to mind (freewriting). Then they return to the place where they stopped writing in their last session and resume writing. The new writing may not dovetail neatly with the old, but the joint can be repaired later.

Some writers will read none of the first draft until a day or two after they have finished it. That way they can see the draft more objectively and start weeding, pruning, planting, and transplanting with a surer hand.

Many writers say that the first draft takes sweat or blood, or both. Other authors believe that they cannot have sex and write well in the same day. To them, writing seems that demanding. For many, after the first draft is on paper—however misshapen and incomplete—the hardest, most exhausting part is done. It's a natural resting point.

9. Rewriting

Basically, my method of writing is rewriting. After I produce a first draft, I'll go over it and cut it. Everything goes that's either redundant or not relevant to the plot or theme. And then I'll go over it again, looking for faulty structure in each sentence; then I'll put it aside and pick it up again a week later to look at all the metaphors, similes—all figurative language—to make sure everything is right. . . . And next I . . . give it to my wife, and she reads it and tells me what she thinks about coherence and believability. Eventually several people see the manuscript and make suggestions, and at some point, I set it aside and let it age like a cheese or something and maybe a month later look at it and see that what I thought was ready to send off to my agent still has a lot of problems, thin spots that need a sentence or two, repetition, faulty connotation—and I go over it again. Sometimes the agent asks for a fix on an obvious problem, and I oblige. (People give advice because they care.) When a magazine editor buys the story, he or she nearly always wants changes, and we work together to make the story as good as we can get it. When the story goes into a collection, another editor asks for more refinements, and we make the story better. And that's a really brief version of what I do to make a story.

> —Tim Gautreaux
> (writer and creative writing professor)

Try again. Fail again. Fail Better.

> —Samuel Beckett

Some Rewriting Techniques

Perhaps eventually you should try all the revising techniques that are explained in this chapter. But don't feel obligated to use them all; that could be overwhelming, even depressing.

Once you have finished the first draft of your story, or have nearly finished it, you should read it aloud. Perhaps do what Samuel Butler did and whenever possible read aloud to someone else: "I always intend to read, and generally do read, what I write aloud to someone; any one almost will do, but he should not be so clever that I am afraid of him. I feel weak places at once when I read aloud where I thought, as long as I read to myself only, that the passage was all right" (Butler 1918, 109).

As you read your story aloud, visualize what is happening in each scene. You might make notes on the copy, but do not interrupt your reading for long. Immediately after reading the story aloud, revise it. Next, put the story aside for at least a day. Then, if possible, get someone else to read it aloud. As the other person reads your story aloud, follow along on another copy and take notes on what might need revision.

Many writers who use a computer believe that it is crucial to print out drafts, read and mark the printouts, then enter those changes on the computer. Garrison Keillor makes a case for doing so: "I write on the laptop and print out a draft; then I pencil in corrections and type them into the computer. It is crucial to put the work in typescript, read it word for word and patch it with a pencil: computer writing tends to be flabby and tone-deaf otherwise" (1999).

After the story has been read aloud and rewritten, you may find it helpful to write a one-paragraph summary of the story; not the story you think you told, but the story you wrote. In one paragraph—no more—describe the essential characters and actions. Write and rewrite this paragraph. The summary should be shorter than your synopsis (if you wrote one) and should describe the story of your first draft.

After you finish the paragraph, consider the following questions:

1. Is the story true to life and not based on television or popular movies?

2. What are the main goals of the major characters? Do we learn of them early in the story?

3. What events help the major characters advance toward the main goals? What prevents progress toward the goals?

4. What does your story show about human motives and behavior?

If you don't like the answers you come up with, revise the story at once.

Save the parts you cut and put them into your journal for possible future mining. The paragraph summary may help you see your story's characterization, structure, and meanings more clearly so that you may rewrite the story and improve it.

Making a list of possibilities is another technique you might try, especially if you think your story is too short or that parts of it are undeveloped. This technique helps you consider alternatives. After you have reread your paragraph summary, quickly jot down brief answers for each of these questions: (1) What other problems might the main character face while pursuing the goals? (2) How would the main character and others react to those new problems? Quickly write down the wild and silly as well as the reasoned and reasonable. Some other time, look at the outcome from this storm of thoughts. Has anything useful washed up?

You may also want to try this strategy: reread each scene, not necessarily in the order they occur in within the story. As you do so, quickly jot down any additional events that might happen in it or what actions might take place instead of the ones in the scene. Write quickly. Do not judge. On another day, look at your notes and decide if you want to follow up on any. These are notes to yourself, most of which you will not use, but tempests sometimes wash up treasures.

As you reread and rewrite your story, check for other aspects. For example, on a card or sheet of paper, make a short list of what you hope to show in your story. With that card or sheet of paper in hand, reread each scene in the story out of order. As you reread each scene, check your list of points. Does each scene show at least one goal on your list? If not, omit the scene, cut part of it, or add to it. (In using this technique, you may discover something else to add to your list, rather than cutting a scene or part of it.)

As you rewrite your story, make sure you never *tell* something when you could *show* it. In "Ribcage," instead of telling the reader that "Mark was angry because Beth didn't want to go to the drive-in and make out," former student Brian Larson shows us: "He barely paused at a stop sign and drove on. The Mustang lurched with his sloppy shift into first. Beth glanced over at him, and he didn't look back. She put on her seatbelt."

Instead of telling us "Pappy has let his house become a mess after his wife's death," Allen Lujan shows us:

> The first thing I noticed when I walked in the house was a strong, unfamiliar odor. The second thing I noticed was the dirty pots and pans that filled the sink and covered the stove. On the counter next

to the sink, I spotted a large pile of watermelon rinds and a bunch of black moldy bananas. He pushed a bunch of papers out of the way so I could put the bag of groceries on the table.

Except for occasional general observations that explain something crucial that cannot be shown, showing is usually more effective. It tends to be more vivid, memorable, and enjoyable than telling.

As you rewrite your story, make sure that you never show *and* tell; just show. For example, consider the following:

> Bob said, "How can you stand living with her?" Raphael ignores the question, turns away from him, and starts unloading the car trunk.

The phrase "ignores the question" is unnecessary because readers can *see* that Raphael is ignoring the question. To point it out is wasteful and may insult some readers.

When you describe a subject, you may show it from a distance, then move readers in closer to see additional significant detail, then closer still. This technique is sometimes called *focal description*. Early in Brian Larson's story, "Ribcage," is an example: "A textbook lay open in front of him. His medium-point Bic pecked at it listlessly. Tiny blue dots and squiggles of ink swarmed around the page numbers."

If you choose the right nouns and verbs, you'll need few adjectives and adverbs. Instead of writing, "An angry Ashley runs quickly from the room," you might write, "Ashley storms from the room." As much as possible, eliminate overused and worn-out phrases, such as "sad but true," "show her true colors," and "stopped dead in his tracks." They are like the canned music we ignore when we hear it in the background at some places of business.

When describing settings and actions, make sure you have put in only significant details. If you mention an object, it should be important to the story. If you describe an object, be sure that what you say about it is important to the story. For example, don't write, "a blue ball" when its color is unimportant; write, "a ball."

Similarly, check to see that you have not described a character's physical appearance in such detail that the description slows down the reader and gives a false sense of the story's pace. You should also usually avoid giving characters similar-sounding names (for example, Fred and Ned, or Jane and June). Why chance confusing the reader?

Certain actions are difficult to present convincingly. For example, it is difficult to describe a person having a heart attack and make readers believe it. It's better to show how people react to such a crisis. Remember, less is often more: sometimes it's better to leave certain actions to the reader's imagination.

Examine your opening paragraphs especially critically. Could they arouse your reader's curiosity? In an earlier draft, "Intruders" (see chapter 5) began this way:

> Breakfast on the patio had become a Saturday morning ritual. Dad's silver mustache flared as he smiled and pulled a chair out for me, then resumed sipping his coffee, and squinting, as he held the sports page up close to his face.
>
> "Morning, Joanie." His shoulders, once rounded and strong, drooped a little beneath his blue faded terry cloth robe, the same one he used to wear when I was little and he'd carry me around through the house like a sack of potatoes.
>
> I caught a familiar whiff of his Old Spice, as I leaned over and planted a kiss on his smooth cheek.
>
> He winked at me as he leaned back in his chair and called to Mom, "Merle, we're waiting for you."

Little in those paragraphs raises any questions, and some of their details prove unimportant in the long run. Notice the difference in the story's opening now:

> "Morning, Joanie. Had breakfast yet?" Mom sat down next to me and gave my hand a big squeeze. Dad took my other hand in his and offered a word of prayer. I closed my eyes and felt the warm sun on my face. The delicious scent of sweet william filled the morning air. Life had returned to normal.
>
> It was then that the phone rang, punctuating Dad's quiet moment of thanksgiving.

This opening shows the family's love and religiosity and nature's warmth and beauty. It then concludes with the sentence, "Life had returned to normal." Most readers will wonder what the problem had been. When the phone rings, "punctuating" the father's prayer and the "quiet moment of thanksgiving," readers will likely want to know who is calling and why and if the call will relate to life returning to normal or upset the normalcy of the happy home. The call, after all, is a break in the quiet and in the mood of thanksgiving. Readers are hooked: they are curious to read on and learn the answers to the questions suggested by the story's opening.

How much rewriting you will need to do is impossible to gauge in advance, but it will probably be much more than you thought when you began. You should work on your rewrites while you are strong and alert. And do so on different days. Remember that most successful writers spend much longer on rewriting than on planning and writing. When you are sure you have done all you can to improve the story, set it aside for a few more days, then reread it, check drawings you have made, check your summary, check your lists, and review the other pointers in this chapter.

If you wrote a synopsis or scene cards, perhaps update them and reread them, too. Chances are that you will see still other ways to improve the story. Don't be surprised if you do, and try not to be impatient to finish.

Story Checklists

[T]he writer who will not revise is a nuisance to himself, his teacher, and to mankind at large. He is also missing what has always been for me the most gratifying part of writing. (Cassill 1975, 19)

After you have written two drafts (or three or four), you may want to use the following selective list of questions to help you decide if your story needs more revision. Don't be surprised, though, if you don't use all these questions. If you try to apply all of them to your story, you could feel overwhelmed.

The most important questions you should ask of your story are about its sources (knowing your subject extremely well) and its specificity (being specific and showing situations, not explaining them in a general manner).

If your story passes the sources and specificity tests, apply some of the following questions to it.

Settings

1. Is the setting of each scene indicated?
2. Have you avoided settings you know only from movies and television shows?

3. For a setting described in detail, is all the detail significant to the story?

4. Does the setting of each scene show something about the character who occupies it?

5. Do some settings, such as a dimly lit room, contribute to the mood of the scene?

6. Do the clothes reveal a character's personality or mood?

Characters

1. What is the main character's goal? Can readers see what it is early in the story? What blocks the character's progress toward that goal?

2. Given the short length of the story, are there too many characters?

3. Are the characters' names easy to remember and distinct from each other?

4. Review your story and underline the actions of your main character. Are they believable?

5. Do you sometimes show a character's reactions to an action rather than showing the action?

Means of Perception, Person, and Tense

1. Have you restricted the reader's access to the mind of only one character, especially within each scene?

2. Have you told all of the story using either first person (an imaginary *I*) or third person *(he, she,* and *they)*?

3. Have you been careful not to shift tense in a confusing manner? For example, the narrator tells the reader that something has happened, then in the next paragraph relates that something is happening?

Dialogue

1. Using a colored pencil or pen, underline all of your main character's dialogue. Then reread that dialogue aloud, including noises such as grunts, snorts, wheezes. Does the dialogue sound true to life and true to the character's personality?

2. Using a pencil or pen of a different color from the one used above, re-

peat the process for another important character. Repeat this process until you have examined the dialogue of each important character.

3. Are silences used to establish a mood, such as tension? Are silences used to convey uncertainty? Are they used to suggest that something is difficult to express in words?

4. Do the characters interrupt each other? Finish each other's sentences? Sometimes trail off without completing thoughts? Effective dialogue often displays these real-life characteristics.

5. Do the characters think to themselves or talk aloud to themselves? In many beginner's stories, the characters do a lot of talking aloud to themselves. In similar situations in life, people usually think. Ask yourself if your characters, when alone, would talk aloud or think.

6. Are there incomplete sentences? Colloquial words? Contractions such as *don't* for *do not*? Speech and dialogue often have all three.

7. a. If a character uses slang, is it used only occasionally to suggest the slang's flavor? To suggest a dialect do you use only occasional words and phrases rather than many phonetic spellings? A full transcription of a character's dialect often makes for tedious or unnecessarily difficult reading.

b. If a character uses swear words, are they used selectively? In spite of the prominence of swear words in popular contemporary movies and music, it can be off-putting, distracting, or counterproductive if you reproduce all the swear words that a person in a similar life situation might use.

Do not try to re-create real speech in its entirety. The dialogue should be selective yet representative and believable.

8. Are meanings hinted at and left unsaid in the dialogue?

9. Are any sentences or passages too long? Good dialogue is more concise than the conversations we hear in life.

10. Do some scenes contain much dialogue but little else? If a lot of dialogue is necessary, consider making the characters move about or do something while they communicate with each other. Whatever they do should fit into the scene and be in character; it should not be busywork.

11. Does each speech convey only one idea or point?

12. Does the dialogue supply information unobtrusively and without insulting the reader's intelligence?

13. Does the dialogue indirectly reveal what the characters are like and what they want? Remember: in life, people are often not forthright.

14. Do those characters who know each other well use their first names only occasionally? In conversations, people who know each other well rarely use each other's first names.

Structure

1. Does the story's opening motivate the reader to read the rest of the story?

2. Can some of the opening be cut? Does the story begin too soon: does the reader need more preparation for the story to come?

3. Does the story cover a week's time or less? (That's a good choice for most short stories.)

4. If flashbacks are used, are they employed only after the reader has become involved in the story? Do they show important comparisons or contrasts between past and present situations? If not, why are you using flashbacks rather than a chronological version of the story?

5. Given the characters and the story's meanings, can any scenes be omitted or shortened?

6. Do any scenes need to be developed?

7. Can scenes be rearranged in a different order to create more effective results?

8. Is there more than one mood in the story?

9. Have you considered using transitions between scenes? Study the transitions in the stories from Part Two. Notice how they can be used to group scenes and to show a change of location or passage of time, or both.

10. Is the ending indeterminate about what might happen next, or does it leave readers with a sense of completeness? Given the story and characters, is the ending justified and believable?

Meanings

Review your story's settings, characters, and structure.

1. What does your story show in general about human behavior?

2. Does your story show the complexity of human nature, such as conflicting emotions or contradictory allegiances?

3. Does the story sometimes explain what is already evident to observant readers? If so, cut the explanation.

Titles

As a rule, a title will come to you—if it comes calling at all—late in the writing process. Certainly, it is nothing to expend precious time and energy on as you write and rewrite the story. Normally, you need to write and rewrite (and rewrite) the story, then see what you have brought forth before you look for a title.

Often the best source is a phrase or image from the story itself. Consider "Crooked Handlebars" (chapter 3). As you review the story, you realize that the crooked handlebars are not merely a damaged part of the man's bicycle. For many readers they also signify something out of alignment, perhaps because of a jarring event. Those associations may also seem to apply to the story's two main characters. Initially, in a sense, they are damaged and out of alignment as well.

Certainly a title needs to be concise and arouse some curiosity. Consider "Intruders" (chapter 5). That's about as short a title as one could come up with. It also suggests a problem right away, which rouses the reader's curiosity: who are the intruders, why do they intrude, and what are the consequences of their intrusion? A lengthy title will probably soon be forgotten, so make the title as short as you can. For example, for a story about a mother who refuses to do her usual duties, instead of "My Mom on Strike," use "Mom on Strike." That title arouses curiosity. The title also suggests someone unhappy with the usual state of affairs, so right away readers wonder why. They are starting to get hooked.

In addition to avoiding titles that arouse no curiosity and those that are unnecessarily long, you should avoid titles that explain too much. For example, a title might unwisely give the author's interpretation of one of the story's main meanings. Thus, "The Wages of Sin" or "Pride Going Before the Fall" are probably too transparent, perhaps even insulting, to many readers. "Before the Fall" might be an effective title, however. It's shorter, evokes the longer and more familiar phrase, and could arouse curiosity: readers know there will be problems for someone in the story and are promised some insight into what led up to the problems or punishment.

Fiction Formats

Before you show your story to others, you should check that it adheres to the following guidelines. Doing so will help readers understand your story with a minimum of interference; it will also demonstrate that you know your business.

Here are some of the conventions that published fiction writers follow:

1. As each new character speaks, begin a new paragraph.

2. If you like, leave an extra blank line or a recurrent symbol (# # # # #, for example) between scenes or groups of scenes, as in "Crooked Handle-

bars." If you prefer, you can number the scenes or groups of scenes, as in "Treason and Vengeance."

3. Use double quotation marks for dialogue; use no quotation marks for thoughts (or set them off with italics or underlining). For example: Ted said, "I will never marry her." Sherry thought, *Don't you believe it,* or, Sherry thought, <u>Don't you believe it</u>.

4. Don't worry about using "he said" or "she said" too often. In this case, the admonition to vary word choice does not apply.

5. When you omit something and use ellipses, include a space before and after each period, as in "Are you sure you. . . ?"

6. Punctuate dialogue as follows:
    a. "_____," he said.
    b. She said, "_____."
    c. "Well," she said, "_____."
    d. "_____?" Alicia asked.

If the context makes it clear who is speaking, omit the "he said" and "she said" tags.

7. You should probably not join possible sentences with commas, although publishers of fiction often allow it.

Do not use: Ted said he would never marry Sherry, she thought that he would.

Instead, use either: Ted said he would never marry Sherry. She thought that he would. Or Ted said he would never marry Sherry, but she thought that he would.

8. The last step in putting your story into its going-out clothes is to make up the title page. No rigid rules dictate its content or format. All you need to do is type the title and place it within quotation marks in the middle of a blank sheet. On the next line or two, type "A Story by [your name]."

After you have recopied your story, read it aloud and make any minor corrections that are necessary.

Reading Aloud in a Group, Getting and Giving Feedback, and Revising

If you think your work is perfect in the first draft, just read it aloud. Listen for the music of your language, and for the false notes and tiresome repetitions. Remember that every word of your fiction should either illuminate the characters or move the story forward. (Wolitzer 1991, 289)

After writing and rewriting a story, many writers rush the story to relatives or friends—and come away from them more convinced than ever that they have written the world's first flawless story! Other writers have relatives or friends who insist that the story is worthless. Unfortunately, rare are the relatives or friends who can read a story with understanding and give you precise and reasoned responses and their suggestions for improving it.

Instead of showing your story to relatives or friends, have a small group read it and mark it up. Next, have each person read the dialogue of one character aloud. Have one person read the descriptions of the settings and the action aloud. Afterward, ask the readers to explain their *responses* to the story. You may want to tape-record the reading and discussion. The best group members not only read their parts with feeling but also have a background in reading stories. The ideal group member also has that elusive but essential characteristic: sound judgment.

Writers need skilled readers to review their drafts because authors are rarely astute critics of their own work. They are too involved or too enthusiastic or too depressed about their work to see it clearly and judge it fairly. Often, readers point out something that the writer was unaware of. That's one reason writers should listen to readers, not explain to them what they tried to convey in the story. As the German philosopher Nietzsche reputedly wrote, the author must keep his mouth shut when his work starts to speak.

After the reading and discussion have run their course, you should collect the readers' notes, revise the story as soon as possible, then take a breather. You should then read the story aloud again and revise further.

Although feedback from readers can be enormously helpful, readers give incomplete and often contradictory advice. Typically, later readings yield new understanding of the story, so keep rereading your story, as long as you are not sick of it, even after you finish considering others' responses. If you continue, however, to reread and rewrite your story after you are tired of it, you will do more harm than good. You may even do major damage. When you start to tire, stop working on the story. Look at it again only after you are rested.

If you plan group readings and discussions, you may want to consult the following checklists, which contain more detailed suggestions than given above.

The Writer

1. You should supply a copy of the completed and revised story to each member of the group at least one day before the group reads the story aloud and gives feedback.

2. As the group reads the story aloud, you should make notes on a copy. Include points to ask the readers after the reading and discussion of the story, corrections to the story, phrases that seem difficult to read smoothly or don't sound right, what readers read instead of what is written, how listeners responded to different parts of the story, and so forth.

3. You should not tell the group the source of the story or your intentions or meanings. If you have brought your child up well, it should be able to speak clearly for itself.

4. Do not tell your group what outside readers said about your writing. Don't say, for example, "I showed this story to three friends, and they said it was wonderful." And, by implication, "Why are you so dense?" Again, the writing should speak for itself.

5. After the group has read the story aloud and given extensive feedback, you should ask questions about parts of the story that still seem to need work. Be sure to take notes on how the group responds to your questions.

To summarize: *in group discussions, the writer should only listen, observe, take notes, and ask questions.*

The Readers

1. Each reader should read the story at least twice and mark questions, comments, and corrections on it before the group reads the story aloud and discusses it.

2. After the story has been read aloud, members should provide many specific and descriptive reactions to it. What did the writing make you think and feel? Why did it do so?

Sweeping and vague judgments such as, "It's great" or "I don't like it" are of little help to the writer and may even be harmful. Much more useful are specific and descriptive reader reactions. For example, "The first scene makes me think of _____." "This character shows that _____." "The story suggests _____ because _____."

To give specific and descriptive reactions, readers might fill in the blanks of this sentence: "This _____ makes me feel/remember/wonder/think _____ because _____." Readers might also ask the writer "What if. . . ?"

questions (What if something else happened, or did not happen, in the story?). One way to keep reader comments specific and descriptive is for group members to reread important passages aloud and tell the writer what the passages make them feel/remember/wonder/think.

3. After the group has given its specific and descriptive reactions and after the group has given the writer a chance to question the group, the group might ask the writer if he or she wants any advice. (If not, that's OK: usually specific and descriptive reactions are much more useful to writers than advice anyway.) If the writer wants advice, it could take this form: "What if you tried this: _____?"

4. Give your positive reactions first. Even an experienced and confident writer may become defensive when faced with an opening barrage of negative comments.

5. Each group member should write notes on the draft—notes that the members give to the writer after the discussion. As someone makes a particularly useful observation or asks an important question, someone else in the group should write it on the draft. For example, one group member might write something like this in the margin: *Debbie asked "Why would the main character quit her job?"*

6. When asked at the right time and in a supportive way, questions are as useful as observations. Sometimes more so.

7. Members of the group should not spend time arguing with each other. Instead, you should concentrate on giving the writer your reactions and your reasons for them. Don't stress a disagreement with another group member; give your reactions to the writer, not to another group member. For example, it's negative and argumentative to say the following to another group member: "You're wrong. That scene does not show _____." Better to say something directly to the writer such as: "To me this scene shows _____." Later, the writer can decide which responses were useful.

8. The writer's autobiography should not be a topic for discussion. Nearly all effective short stories contain some fact and some fiction, but it's unimportant which parts are which. Do not assume that a character is based on the writer. Might be; might not. Besides, in terms of the story, what does it matter?

9. If one person begins to dominate the group discussion, other group members should speak more often.

10. If the discussion comes to a halt, wait a while. If the discussion still lags, the writer might ask questions about parts of the story . Or the writer

could ask group members to reread and respond to a scene that does not seem effective.

11. It's not worth a group's time and energy to discuss spelling, punctuation, or capitalization. Any such issues should be noted on the copy of the draft that will be returned to the writer after the discussion.

To summarize: *In group discussions the emphasis should be on the writing, not the writer, and the feedback should be specific, descriptive, and—at least sometimes—positive.*

If you have read and written little fiction, please heed the following advice. In group discussion of a story's narrator and characters, the writer should avoid using *I, me, mine, we, us,* and *our.* The readers should avoid *you* and *your.* Instead, use *she, he, her, his, they,* and *their.* By doing so, you are keeping the focus on *fiction.*

Before you apply these guidelines to discussing a draft written by someone in your group, it might be a good idea for your group to practice reading and giving feedback on one or more of the stories in chapters 3–5.

Sample Feedback

In the Margins

The following sample marginal notes are ones that I wrote for a set of short stories. The notes suggest what the writers might omit or rewrite, and they let the writer know what the reader notices (and in some cases enjoys or appreciates).

Omit (in brackets)

1. How does this fit into the story? *or* Is this important to the story? *or* Can you prune any of this?

2. Omit this here and let us figure this out later?

3. We can tell already. *or* We can well imagine this. *or* We need not be told.

4. Omit? We have already seen this.

5. Show us, and let readers make the judgment. ("He was a little less diplomatic.")

6. Do you want a pause here? (a comma that need not be included unless the writer wants readers to pause briefly in the reading)

7. Too obviously a message (and brackets around a group of generalized sentences that explain aspects of the story unnecessarily)

8. This scene begins slowly: no tension, humor, or sex. Cut the begin-

ning and begin later in the scene? (earlier scenes established that the story is partly about a sexual relation)

9. Redundant (brackets mean consider omitting): extended [out], reverted [back], also . . . [as well], swayed [gently] in a light breeze, herded [like cattle] onto the bus, thought [to herself], a [brief] moment, and countless others.

10. Would he? (for characters speaking aloud to himself, though most people rarely do)

11. Where else? (for "His heart began to pound [in his chest].")

12. The narrator judges too often. Let the reader discover and decide.

13. Omit (a) Fred gets into his car[, and they continue to talk]. "Do you ever think about us?" she asks. (b) Finally, [exasperated to violence,] she lashed out sharply with her foot, [shouting,] "I'm sick of this. Now get the hell out of here!"

14. What he says next *shows* this.

Rewrite, or Rewrite and Add Details

15. Show us. Don't tell us. ("became a living nightmare," "I was not at all happy about this new friendship," and "I was quickly losing my temper")

16. Just use "said."

a. This *shows* it's a greeting: "Hey, glad you guys could make it," greeted Jim. Change *greeted* to *said*.

b. We can tell it's repeated: "No way," Bob said. "Yeah, no way," repeated Teressa. Change *repeated* to *said*.

17. Is this what you mean? (for a word that doesn't fit in)

18. Show us at least some of this. ("The pain of the past months had taken her to her breaking point.")

19. This is a lot of telling. Can you show some of this later? (for a paragraph of generalizations)

20. Use a verb instead?

have a feeling —> think

had a tendency —> tended

makes an agreement —> agrees

21. overused phrase ("the soft breeze," "butterflies in my stomach")

22. vague word ("magnificent")

23. Would they? (for something out of character that two characters did)

24. Can you tell us less and show us more? ("a poster's beauty and power had captured the child's imagination")

25. I cannot see this.

26. How so? You need to be more specific (someone runs "making plenty of noise").

27. In what sense? I cannot see this clearly. (for "a broken iron gate" Does it sag? Does it drag? Does it have a broken lock? Is it hard to open and close? Does it look misshapen? Amusing? Is it rusted, too? Peeling?)

28. The story *tells* us so much there's little for readers to discover and thereby become involved with.

Reactions to Story Developments

29. Because she did _____ in the second scene, I was surprised to see her do _____ here.

30. I've been expecting this development since the first scene when _____.

31. I laughed aloud here.

32. I smiled as I read this.

33. It doesn't make sense to me that he would _____ here because _____.

34. I've been curious about what he would do if she _____.

Praise or Reassurance

35. Effective short reply.

36. This creates curiosity (a scene ends, "Wade stands and smiles as he views the contents" but only later in the story do readers learn what the contents were).

37. Amusing (so the writer knows when I smiled or laughed)

38. He doesn't answer her question (this shows the writer I noticed this)

39. Helpful (or vivid) detail:

    a. "When she looked at him, she had to take one step back to get a clear, full view." This *shows* she's small and he's big.

    b. [during a meal] "Edward asked [a question] through his napkin"

40. I can see this (for a particularly vivid description) or vivid details.

41. Imaginative comparison ("When the vehicle was unloaded, it rested like an insect carcass under a huge mango tree.")

On the Story Itself

As is explained earlier in this chapter, the best way for readers to help writers is for readers to describe specific responses they had while reading a story. Writers will be able to use the reader's explanations about where the story was surprising, where sections were too predictable or even boring, where the story was confusing, where amusing, where sad, what the major characters were like, what seems symbolic, what the story reveals about human behavior in general, and so forth. It also helps writers to know how readers reacted during the first reading and how their reactions changed during a later reading.

One productive way to give feedback is to proceed through a story, commenting on the ways in which the story affected you as you read it. To illustrate this method of giving feedback, below I have described some of my reactions to "Crooked Handlebars." Before reading the following feedback, please reread that story or review it carefully (pp. 35–44).

The story's first sentence and first paragraph both arouse my curiosity and incline me to read further. Why does the first-person narrator (we later learn that he is called "Nick") have a gurgling and churning stomach; is he upset or hungry, or both, or is there some other cause? Why was he beaten up? Why did the narrator lie to his best friend about the source of the bruise? The story begins with an effective hook: I wanted to read on and find answers.

In the third paragraph, when the narrator says, "I had never stole a bike before," that phrase could have at least two meanings. Here, I wonder if Nick's statement means no more than it says on the surface or if it means that he has stolen other things. That he has "seen Macky's older brother" steal a bicycle twice reveals that the narrator hangs out with boys who break the law.

The description of the man consists of many details that I cannot appreciate until later in the story or until a second reading (that is not a problem). In the fourth and fifth paragraphs, for example, we learn that the man "had big bloodshot eyes," which made me wonder if he drinks too much, has been grieving, has been crying because of his own ill health or some other major frustration, has not been getting his rest, or something else, but at any rate all is not well with him, and I wonder why. His "stubby beard" means he's not trimming it; he's not shaving, not taking care of his appearance. "His strong body odor" also suggests he's neglecting himself. Again, during the first reading, I wonder why. Later in the story, I learn that this man has bloodshot eyes, stubby beard, and strong body odor because he is grieving, not sleeping well, is drinking heavily, and is not bathing and grooming himself.

When the man calls the boy "thief," he does so spontaneously; later, nearly everything the man says to Nick is calculated, by turns to test him, worry him, or try to win his trust and friendship. When the man says, "I could have sworn that I parked my bike a little closer to the wall," and "I guess it must have rolled a little," he may be testing the boy, to see how he will react, or he may want to make the boy feel uncomfortable. He may have both motives.

The man's questions about the boy's bruise and about whether he has told his parents show that the man has some interest in the boy's welfare. The boy's answers supply some important and unobtrusive exposition: his mom lives in another town (she's evidently separated or divorced); the boy lives with his dad, who may be away for a few days (evidently the father beat the boy). At any rate, the boy seems to be on his own. So far, I'm thinking that the boy is getting into trouble: getting beat up, trying to steal, and lacking parental support and supervision.

At about this point, we begin to see what a shrewd psychologist the man is. I think he wants to get to know the boy at least a little better but sees that he is skittish, so the man says he is having trouble with the bike now that it has fallen and has "crooked handlebars," and he would appreciate the boy's carrying the bag of groceries. (There's justice in the boy helping out anyway; he damaged the man's bike while trying to steal it.) The first section of the story ends with another significant detail: the man has a liquor bottle sticking out of his back pocket. This is the first of many clues that the man is drinking heavily.

When they arrive at the man's house, the boy is still eager to leave, but the man says the right things to get him to stay. Finally, we learn the two characters' names: Nick and Pappy. Note that the man had asked some questions of the boy but had not asked his name; the man was more interested in the boy himself. The man's name, "Pappy," is a diminutive and usually affectionate version of *father,* and by the end of the story he will be on his way to becoming Nick's substitute for the abusive father.

For the first of many times in the story, we hear about Pappy's boat; we learn that it is "dirt- and dust-covered"; in other words, it hasn't been used in a long time. A few paragraphs later we figure out why: Pappy tended his wife in all but her last two days and has been grieving "a couple of weeks" since her death. He's had no time or desire to go boating and fishing.

As Pappy and Nick enter Pappy's backyard, Pappy again puts some psychological pressure on Nick, as he stares at him unsmilingly and says that not long ago his dogs chewed up a thief and that they "have supersensitive sniffers and get real mean when they corner a thief." In part, I suspect Pappy wants to punish Nick, make him suffer for trying to steal and, perhaps, for damaging Pappy's bicycle. I notice, too, that Pappy refers to his dogs as "my boys" and later says his wife "took care of these boys just like they were her own kids." Pappy has no children. Nothing in the story leads me to believe he has family. For that matter, we get no clues he has friends. Until Nick comes Pappy's way, he seems cut off from human contact.

We see that Nick is ambivalent when Pappy offers him a meal: Nick "took a few steps then stopped." We do not need to be told the next sentence: "I was hungry, but I didn't know if I could trust Pappy." We've been shown; we need not be told.

By its choice of details about the setting, the next section of the story reveals much about Pappy and Mamo's happy days together (dancing, fishing, bowling), about Mamo's last days, and about Pappy's days since then. Pappy neglects not only himself but also the house: it's a mess. Some of the feeling resulting from Mamo's loss is also suggested by the many images of quiet and isolation and by that odor that's new and strange to Nick.

Significantly, "a bed that looked like it belonged in a hospital" is "in the middle of the room, without any sheets or blankets." There is also a wheelchair and walker, "three pillows without slips," and two TV trays, one with "a water pitcher and several plastic cups, all empty and turned upside down." Other resonant details are the plastic prescription bottles, a Bible, get-well cards, and photographs of antique cars. These photographs depict another passion of Pappy's that he has put aside. These and other details all help me see what it looks like inside Pappy's house, but they also establish a mood of loss and loneliness.

Some details are easy to overlook. For example, at first Pappy offers Nick "steaks and eggs" (p. 39), but later he serves him "scrambled eggs, cut up weenies, and a couple of flour tortillas" (p. 41). Did Pappy lie or exaggerate, or did he forget or change his mind? We cannot know, though we may have an opinion on the matter.

In the story's next section, we learn Pappy is still drinking rum and Cokes, and "his eyes were still red, and he looked tired," but he revives somewhat when he shares one of his pleasures in life with Nick, his antique Model-A. Like the boat, Pappy's driving cap is covered with dust; Pappy has not driven the car in a long time.

The next section describes the visit to the cemetery. Again, the story shows restraint. We do not see Pappy at Mamo's grave, except from a distance and in the fading light. After Pappy returns to the car, Nick says, "I couldn't tell for sure, but I think he had been crying." We often do not get to know for certain what Pappy is thinking and feeling, but then all we can know is what Nick tells us. He is our only source.

In the next section, Pappy's mood has brightened as he drives his antique car down Main Street, but again the author has added words that tell me what I have already seen. People are waving and staring at Pappy and Nick as they drive along, so we need not be told "The old car received quite a bit of attention."

Pappy is about to say goodbye to Nick and hopes to see him again. So what does he do? He thanks him and compliments him. When Pappy says "I have a feeling that whoever hit you in the face isn't going to go away," he is showing that he knows Nick has been in trouble and remains at risk. Pappy hastens to add that he knows Nick can take care of himself (Nick announced as much early in the story) but, "just in case, I want you to know you can always come see me." Finally, Pappy invites Nick on a fishing trip.

Pappy is a fisherman, all right. He is angling for a new friend, but one false move and the fish might wriggle away. Pappy is skillful, and Nick is hooked (or about to be). Significantly, in the penultimate paragraph and, for the first time, Nick calls the man "Pappy." With Pappy, Nick can have new experiences: have a dog, go boating and fishing, drive around in an exotic car and be waved at, and, most of all, have a pappy who is concerned about his welfare, smiles at him, shares with him generously, and enjoys his company. With Nick, Pappy also has much to gain. To move beyond his grief, nurturing a young person may be the best therapy. In helping Nick, Pappy can begin putting death, dust, and disorder behind him and gain a new friend, fishing partner, and, most of all, a new family. "The boys," Feather and Charlie Brown, are not enough.

"Crooked Handlebars" shows all this, and more, with little telling—and does so with subtlety, lots of believable detail, and complexity but with no sentimentality.

Summary and Conclusion

Talent is long patience.

> —attributed to Gustave Flaubert

1. Do writing exercises and write journal entries as you read and study short stories.

2. Base your stories on your own experiences or those you know extremely well.

3. Use different names for your characters than the names of the sources for the characters. Make some changes in the events and in the order of the events so that you will begin to think in terms of characters and fiction, not people and facts.

4. Rarely begin a story with a long description of a setting. Instead, begin by hooking the reader. Look at the opening paragraphs of stories in a recent collection of short stories. Usually, they arouse the reader's curiosity. Many of them begin in the middle of a scene.

5. Build your story in terms of scenes: more or less continuous action in one location. Try making scene cards before or after your first draft.

6. Carefully consider the use of flashbacks. If you do use them, consider introducing them with the past-perfect tense; then shift to the past tense. For example, "Jill had fretted all day. She had been distracted by Juan's response. She worried. . ."

7. Limit your story to one means of perception: let readers see inside the mind of only one character.

8. In general, the shorter the story, the shorter the story time. Remember, too, that short stories typically cover only a few days or a few scenes from a few weeks.

9. Do not try to write and rewrite at the same time. Finish your first draft, then rewrite it. Take a break. Then read your draft aloud and rewrite it.

10. After you finish your first draft and begin to rewrite your story, consider the main options for showing characters:

direct analysis (use sparingly)

significant action

dialogue

thoughts (of one character)

appearance *(significant* detail)

    character's physical characteristics, gestures, clothing

    things the character owns

    where the character lives or works

11. After the first or second draft, for all sections that do not seem right, ask "What if. . . ?" What if the character did this next, then that, and that? What would be the consequences?

12. Often you can make the best beginning by chopping off the first paragraph (or even a page or so).

13. Often you can make the best ending by stopping at a point that is one or two paragraphs earlier than you first thought.

14. Be careful that neither the narrator nor one of the characters explains the story's meanings.

15. Usually show, don't tell. Let your readers discover. For example, don't tell us Sarah is angry; show her being angry.

Summary of the Summary

1. Know your subject well. Each of your early stories should be heavily based on your own experiences. Later stories may be based on someone else's experiences that you know thoroughly.

2. Let your readers see and hear believable human experience.

3. Wherever possible, show your subject without telling readers about it (for example, "Jan scowled and replied in a tight voice," not "Jan was angry").

4. Don't explain the story's significance or meanings. Let your readers figure out what is what.

5. Specificity. Specificity. Specificity.

By planning, writing, and rewriting your short stories, you will develop story-writing skills, gain the satisfaction of sharing your vision of life, and achieve the rewards of reaching others. And, if you like, you'll be in better condition for writing novels. After you have learned to run miles, you may be ready for a marathon.

Appendix

Glossary

Works Cited

Index

Appendix

Tips on Publishing

Writing the story may have been challenging and satisfying, but it was written for others to see and hear what you had in mind, and you should work to see your best short stories published.

If you decide to try to publish, one possible outlet is a college or university literary magazine. Find out the deadline for the next issue and get a copy of the rules for submission.

By checking one or more of the three reference works described below, then examining issues of the magazines that they describe, you might locate magazines that would be interested in your stories.

The International Directory of Little Magazines and Small Presses (Len Fulton, ed., Paradise, Calif.: Dustbooks). For the latest edition of this source, see your local library. Information is listed for thousands of magazines and book publishers. For each are given the publication name, editor, address, phone number, subscription information, types of submissions welcomed, and forms of payment. It also includes an extensive subject index.

Novel and Short Story Writer's Market (Cincinnati: Writer's Digest Books) and *Writer's Market* (Cincinnati: Writer's Digest Books). These two annual reference works cover the types of writings that book publishers and magazine editors are seeking, how much they may pay, and often the names of specific editors to write. Also included is information about agents, how to submit materials, and kinds of rights (for example, first serial, all rights, or syndication rights). A glossary and an index conclude each volume. Nearly all public and academic libraries own a copy of the latest edition of *Writer's Market*; some have *Novel and Short Story Writer's Market*.

Once you discover a particular magazine that might consider your story for publication, you may find the following suggestions of use:

1. Make sure that you have consistently followed the fiction formats (pp. 112–13).

2. Type or print out your final draft on white bond paper.

3. Put page numbers at either the top or the bottom of each sheet, but be consistent in their placement.

4. Put the story's title at the top left of each sheet.

5. Make at least one photocopy or computer backup copy of your story.

6. Do not staple or paper-clip the pages together.

7. Send your story in a plain manila envelope.

8. If you want the copy of your story returned (in case it is rejected), enclose a stamped, self-addressed manila envelope. If you do not do so, you may never see that copy again.

9. Often you need send no cover letter, but if you do, make it brief and factual. Do not boast about yourself or your achievements, and do not explain or justify the story. Do briefly tell what you are sending, about how long it is, and how you can be reached (include your e-mail address, if you have one).

If you submit the story to more than one publication at a time, you should let each magazine know this. The latest editions of the annual *International Directory of Little Magazines and Small Presses* and the *Novel and Short Story Writer's Market* may tell you if a magazine accepts multiple submissions. If a magazine you hope to publish in does not accept multiple submissions, you should send your story to only that magazine until you have received a decision.

After you send your story, don't dawdle by your mailbox. A response will probably be much longer in coming than you think is reasonable and it will probably show up when you least expect it. If, after a month or two, you have not heard from the magazine, write and ask the editor when you can expect a decision. If you receive no response after an additional delay, write and ask that your manuscript be returned to you.

On rejections: don't expect editors who reject your story to give you suggestions or encouragement. Usually they are too busy. Do expect rejection slips, few of them personalized. Rejections are a fact of the writer's life. Writing is competitive; editors have different tastes; your story may arrive at an inopportune time (for example, perhaps the magazine has recently accepted a similar story); your story may not be publishable. I repeat:

rejections are a fact of the writer's life. Accept that, or forget about being published.

When a story is rejected and returned, inspect all the pages of the copy. If they are OK, send the manuscript to another publication on the same day. Make a record of the person to whom you send it and when; then move on to other work. Whatever you do, don't dwell on rejections.

Glossary

anecdote: Brief entertaining story that lacks the development, complexity, and subtlety of effective fiction.

character biography: Description of a character's imaginary life before the story, during the story, and perhaps after the story; written by some authors to help them understand their characters more completely.

closure: By the end of the story, the consequences of previous major actions that are shown or clearly implied.

exposition: Information about characters and events that take place before the beginning of the story but are supplied within a story; helps the reader understand the characters or follow the story.

flashback: One or more scenes that interrupt a story to show something that happened in the past.

freewriting: Spontaneous writing with minimal concern for grammar and spelling; used by many writers to generate material that may be rewritten and incorporated into stories later.

hook: Story beginning that entices readers to read further.

meaning: Observation or generalization about a subject; conveyed by explicit statement or, more often, by symbolic object or actions in the story itself.

narrative: An account of a series of related events; more loosely: a story.

pace: Reader's sense of a story moving rapidly or slowly; a highly subjective experience, influenced by such aspects as speed and variety of action and how often new or important information is revealed.

plot: Selection and order of a story's events.

satire: Method of depicting a subject, usually human behavior, in an amusing yet critical way.

scene: Portion of a story that gives the impression of continuous action taking place in continuous space.

scene card: Note card or piece of paper that is used to briefly describe a scene's setting, characters, or action; often used to plan a story or to prepare for revising a draft.

setting: Location of a scene; where the action takes place; often used to reveal or enhance character, mood, or meanings.

story line: Story about a character or a few characters; short stories tend to have only one, but novels often have two or more.

story time: Amount of time covered by a story (for example, if the earliest scene occurs on a Sunday and the latest scene takes place on the following Tuesday, the story time is three days).

structure: Selection and arrangement of the parts of a whole; in a short story, it can be thought of as the selection and arrangement of scenes; in stories, the actions are not necessarily chronological, and insignificant actions are omitted.

subject: Characters, objects, or ideas in a story (for example, the three subjects of "Treason and Vengeance" are a young woman and two young men).

symbol: Any perceptible object that has significance or meaning beyond its usual meaning or function; depending on context, a sound, word (including a name), color, action, or something else which the senses may perceive could all function as symbols.

theme: See *meaning*.

Works Cited

Beckett, Samuel. 1992. "Worstward Ho" in *Nohow On,* 101. London: Calder.

Brande, Dorothea. 1981. *Becoming a Writer.* Los Angeles: J. P. Tarcher.

Butler, Samuel. 1918. "On the Making of Music, Pictures and Books." *The Note-Books of Samuel Butler.* London: A. C. Fifield.

Cassill, R. V. 1975. *Writing Fiction,* 2d ed. Englewood Cliffs, N.J.: Prentice Hall.

Crichton, Robert. 1982. "Across the River and Into the Prose." In *Creativity and the Writing Process,* edited by Olivia Bertagnolli and Jeff Rackham 152–63. New York: John Wiley & Sons.

Egri, Lajos. 1960. *The Art of Dramatic Writing: Its Basis in the Creative Interpretation of Human Motives.* New York: Simon and Schuster.

Elbow, Peter. 1981. *Writing with Power: Techniques for Mastering the Writing Process.* New York: Oxford Univ. Press.

Engle, Paul. 1982. "Salt Crystals, Spider Webs, and Words." In *Creativity and the Writing Process,* edited by Olivia Bertagnolli and Jeff Rackham, 49–57. New York: John Wiley & Sons. Quoting Anton Chekhov.

Gautreaux, Tim. 1997. "All Things Considered." *National Public Radio.* December 15. <http://www.npr.org/programs/atc/archives/971215.atc.html> The excerpt quoted was derived from the NPR interview, then edited by Mr. Gautreaux.

Holman, Sheri. 1999. "How I Write." *The Times* (London), 13 Nov.

Huddle, David. 1982. "Memory's Power." In *Creativity and the Writing Process,* edited by Olivia Bertagnolli and Jeff Rackham, 103–12. New York: John Wiley & Sons.

Hugo, Richard. 1979. *The Triggering Town: Lectures and Essays on Poetry and Writing.* New York: W. W. Norton.

Hull, Raymond. 1983. *How to Write a Play.* Cincinnati: Writer's Digest Books.

Johnson, Dirk. 1986. "A Storytelling Renaissaance." *New York Times,* 19 May.

Keillor, Garrison. 1999. "How I Write." *The Times* (London), 4 Dec.

Knight, Damon. 1985. *Creating Short Fiction.* Revised ed. Cincinnati: Writer's Digest Books.

Lamott, Anne. 1994. *Bird by Bird: Some Instructions on Writing and Life.* New York: Doubleday. Lamott also writes an on-line diary that has appeared on a cultural webzine at <http://www.salon.com>.

Loch, Chuck. 1981. "How to Feed Your Brain and Develop Your Creativity." *Writer's Digest,* February, 20–22, 24–25.

Macrorie, Ken. 1980. *Telling Writing.* 3rd ed. Rochelle Park, N.J.: Hayden.

McLaren, John. 1999. "How I Write." *The Times* (London), 11 Dec.

Minot, Stephen. 1998. *Three Genres: The Writing of Poetry, Fiction, and Drama.* 6th ed. Upper Saddle River, N.J.: Prentice Hall.

Neeld, Elizabeth. 1986. *Yes! You Can Write.* Chicago: Nightingale-Conant Corporation.

Oates, Joyce Carol. 1999. "Writers on Writing: to Invigorate Literary Mind, Start Moving Literary Feet." *New York Times,* 18 July. [A list of all the articles in the series "Writers on Writing," and links to them, can be found at <http://www.nytimes.com/books/specials/writers.html>.]

O'Connor, Flannery. 1969. "Writing Short Stories." *Mystery and Manners.* New York: Farrar, Straus & Giroux.

Piercy, Marge. 1999. "Life of Prose and Poetry—an Inspiring Combination." *New York Times,* 20 Dec.

Rule, Rebecca and Susan Wheeler. 1993. *Creating the Story: Guides for Writers.* Portsmouth, N.H.: Heinemann.

Smith, Dinitia. 1999. "Eyes Covered but Seeing, a Novelist Looks Inward." *New York Times,* 1 Dec.

Smith, Dinitia. "Writers as Plunderers: Why Do They Give Away People's Secrets?" *New York Times,* 24 Oct.

Stevens, William K. 1989. "For Those Who Have Lost Sleep, the First Casualty Is Creativity." *New York Times,* 5 Jan.

"Talk on Train Traps Suspect in a Shooting." 1985. *New York Times,* 6 Feb.

Wolitzer, Hilma. 1991. "Twenty Questions." In *Writers on Writing,* edited by Robert Pack and Jay Parini, 281–91. Hanover, N.H.: Middlebury College Press.

Index

Allen, Woody, 22
Anecdotes, 9–10
"Annie B. and Oscar Hodges"
    (journal entry), 23–25

Beckett, Samuel, 103
Beginnings of stories, 74, 82, 107–8,
    120, 124, 125
Brande, Dorothea, 101
Butler, Samuel, 104

Cassill, R. V., 108
Character biographies, 89
Characters in stories, 77–78, 84,
    106; checklist questions about,
    109; in "Crooked Handlebars,"
    120–23
Checklists for stories, 108–11
Chekhov, Anton, 82
Clothing in stories, 77, 109
"Convert, The" (journal entry),
    25–26
Copyright law, 95–96
Cornwell, Melinda, 27
Crichton, Robert, 1, 74
"Crooked Handlebars" (short story),
    35–44; characters and goals in,
    77; feedback on, 120–23; journal

entries for, 33–34; meaning in,
    83; mirroring life, 74; past tense
    in, 79; range of emotions in, 82;
    resolution of, 78; setting off
    groups of scenes in, 112–13;
    settings to reveal characterization,
    76; showing instead of telling,
    105–6; source of title for, 112;
    story time of, 82; title of, 112

Dialogue in stories, 80–81; checklist
    questions about, 109–10
Díaz, Rosa María, 46; interview with,
    55–56
Discovery drafts, 91–92; questions to
    ask about, 92
Doctorow, E. L., 101
Dogs as characters in stories, 8
Doud, Claire, 57; interview with,
    69–70

Egri, Lajos, 77–78
Elbow, Peter, 101
Endings of stories, 82, 83, 111, 123,
    125
Engle, Paul, 82
Exercise: physical, 12–13. *See also*
    Writing exercises

Oates, Joyce Carol, 12, 13
Obscenity and profanity in stories, 5, 110
Obviousness in stories, 75–76
O'Connor, Flannery, 97

Person (first, second, and third point of view), 79, 99; checklist question about, 109
Photographs as sources for writing, 15–16
Piercy, Marge, 83, 100
Point of view. *See* Means of perception
Profanity and obscenity in stories, 5, 110

Rahl, Stacy, 101
Readers, consideration of, 74–76
"Ribcage" (short story), 105, 106
Rule, Rebecca, 79

Scene cards, 93–94; for short story "Intruders," 70–73
Settings, 76–77, 84; checklist questions about, 108–9
Sex in stories, 5
Shakespeare, William, 77
Short stories: characters, 77–78; dialogue, 80–81; limitations and possibilities of meanings, 83–84; means of perception, person, and tense, 78–79; settings, 76–77; structure, 81–83
Showing instead of telling, 105–6, 111, 122, 123, 125
Silence in stories, 110
Slang in stories, 110
Smith, Dinitia, 95, 99
Sonnets and short stories, comparison of, 84
Steele, Sir Richard, 31

Stevens, William K., 12
"Stranded" (journal entry), 18–19
Structure of stories, 78, 79 fig. 2, 81–83, 84; checklist questions about, 111, 124
Subtlety in stories, 75–76, 122, 123
Swanson, Steve, 80
Swear words, 110
Symbols, 94
Synopses, 92–93

Tense of narration, 79; checklist questions about, 109
Themes in stories. *See* Meanings in stories
Time in short stories, 82, 111, 124
Title page, format for, 113
Titles for short stories, 111–12
"Treason and Vengeance" (short story), 47–55; character and goals in, 77; ending of, 81; lighting to establish mood in, 76; main character in, 78; mirroring life, 74; present tense use in, 79; story time of, 82; third person point of view in, 79

Ueland, Brenda, 85
Unconscious as a source for writers, 100–101

Violence in stories, 5–6

"What if...?" playing, 89–91, 125
Wheeler, Susan, 79
Wilson, Lisa, 21
Wolitzer, Hilma, 113–14
Writing exercises, 15–17

Yeats, William Butler, 85